Nostalgia for Unknown Cities

Nostalgia
for
Unknown Cities

Ken Edwards

REALITY STREET
2007

Published by
Reality Street Editions
63 All Saints Street, Hastings, East Sussex TN34 3BN
www.realitystreet.co.uk

Printed & bound in Great Britain by CPI Antony Rowe

Reality Street Narrative Series No 5

A catalogue record for this book is available from the
British Library

ISBN: 978-1-874400-40-0

ACKNOWLEDGEMENTS
"City of Reclamation" was first published in *Golden
Handcuffs Review*.
"City Break" was first published in *Poetry Salzburg Review*.
"Bruised Rationals" in an earlier version was published in
RWC and also used as a text for an orchestral piece by the
author, performed by the London COMA Ensemble.
A shorter version of "City on the Marshes" was first
published in *Kiosk*, and edited extracts as a field report in
Ecopoetics.
My thanks to the various editors, and to Gordon and Sasha
for providing the space in which the bulk of "City of Grain
Elevators" was written. *KE*

Contents

Preface

THE PROTAGONIST, charged with an unwelcome task, remembers the city of his birth, but the memories are no longer reliable. A considerable time later, he wakes from a dream which he recalls only dimly as having something to do with this. There's no clear reason why this should be so: in the dream, which was located in the realm of dreams that bears no obvious resemblance to any actual city that may exist or might have existed, there were large computer screens (perhaps mounted on the sides of buildings) on which endless texts scrolled, changing too fast to permit deciphering; also, land reclamation and underground passages figured, but exact topographical references were not obtainable. The unwelcome task, should it have existed (and there is some doubt about this too), involved taking the ashes of his recently deceased father on a plane journey to be buried in that city, which is also his father's birthplace: the plastic urn provided by the funeral directors, carried as cabin baggage and stowed in the overhead compartment of the aircraft, a source, naturally, of anxiety for the duration of the journey. It isn't the origin of this project, but auto-confirms it.

The starting point is the first person, that arbitrary signifier for the whole concatenation of processes and functions that we call the self: the pandemonium, the "heap or collection of different perceptions, unified together by certain relations" (Hume). And in the unfolding of these accounts very soon the first drifts into the second and then the third, in a semi-rigorous pursuit of objectivity. But if there is some scientific pretension about the accounts, just what is being claimed here? It may be a proposition of these texts that cities dissolve the myriad fleeting selves of which they are composed, that, paradoxically, in so doing they counter also the individual terror of annihilation and lead perhaps to new models of consciousness.

Starting from a different origin, then, the protagonist is returned to contemplation of the unknowable complexities of the city in which he has spent the greater part of his life by far. But the memories of this are no more substantial than those of that other city (that of his birth), and he fears he has already started to lose them. From his new vantage point, outside of it and them, he recognises them for what they are, aspects of that oh so familiar collective dream in which we all partake, which must too soon utterly vanish.

This leads him, then, into considering all the cities

in which he has ever spent time – whether it be a day, three weeks or more than half a life – and indeed those in which he has never set foot but whose hidden corners and by-ways he has fantasised about, cities which may no longer exist or may never have existed – and to attempt to catalogue the experiences within some kind of implicit framework.

Much of his effort goes into forestalling the premature narratives that arise, unwanted and unsought, and yet this quickly reveals itself as an impossible task, as impossible as the original task that gave rise to the project, because try as he may, rearranging the sentences in whatever arbitrary form or order, whether just as they fall in chronological sequence, or in alphabetical sequence, or by length, or other taxonomy, a narrative reimposes itself as a by-product of the experiment, as inexorably as the time that passes. But a narrative whose end is uncertain and unpredictable, where nothing is resolved because everything already is.

1 City of Reclamation

ABOUT 3AM I awoke from a dream of the city in which I was born; and I recalled that I had actually revisited the city, though not for many years after I had first exiled myself from it; but the dream seemed more real than the visit. Above the space created by the dream, a mediaeval tower loomed, overlooking the prison yard, where occasionally you could see prisoners performing sweeping-up chores, and volumes of white sheets on a washing line. A cock began to crow in that early hour. All afternoon, my parents would lean side by side, arms folded and touching each other at the window, gazing down through the slanting shutters at teeming street life below: tradespeople following the dictates of commerce, families promenading, soldiers and sailors, cars, vans and bicycles, stray dogs and idlers – an unwitting precursor of reality television, perhaps. An irrevocable event occurred around that time, which meant that I could never return to the city; or to put it another way, if I were to return I would be so changed that it would not be the same I; or alternatively, had I remained I, then the city would have turned out to be a different city entirely. And so back up the hill, leaving the town area, I passed the house in which we once lived, the one we moved to later, now shuttered (but the same yellow stucco, and riotous bougainvillea over-tumbling the wall from the mysterious garden next door where a hierarchy of cats would play out their opera in the depth of the night). Animals, eroticism, food and artefacts all played a role in my dream of the city. As I review these sentences, it becomes increas-ingly difficult to separate the dream accounts from "real memories".

As LAND had been reclaimed from the sea within the port area in recent years, the urban zone had spread westwards (much later, I was to write, addressing the evanescent self: "But you my beauty who find yourself in a place / vastly crammed with incident and resource, and see / no way out of it, you do not know it. / You venture onto 'reclaimed land' but it's dark to you: // ahead, huge buildings with screens on which luminous text / scrolls & forever transforms, yet seems hardly to change."). As we were conducting the argument, at a street corner, a man passed by with a lion cub on a lead (but this may have happened in a different city entirely). At night, the hills across the bay were dotted with faint electric glows, but the dark sea barely returned the starlight. At the yacht club, people sat

And so back up the hill, leaving the town area, I passed the
house in which we once lived.

talking, reminiscing for hours, drinking and eating kebabs until it was dark. At this point, I had been absent from the city for some thirty years; and so I was astonished at the number of people who appeared still to know me. At weekends, the city was almost deserted as people took to their cars and drove out to picnic in the hinterland that had once been wild, either fishing coast or oak forest, but now, with its endless golf courses and hotels, increasingly resembled the environment they may have wished, consciously or not, to escape. Bastions remained proud. Bathing took place in a familiar atmosphere; cheap goods were available. (Before long, we shall be back on the aircraft and all of this will be forgotten.) Below ground, however, it was said an anti-city existed of paved tunnels, circuses, embrasures, vaults, futuristic hospitals for avant-garde surgery, endless kitchens, tubular structures, ducts of all kinds, locked cabinets, vast and echoing garages, all long since abandoned to the night, its reality denied by day-to-day pedestrians. Beside the swimming-pool, the ghost of an iguana. Beyond these intervals, lemon and olive groves might cover summer-browned slopes, out of present vision. Big buildings – some gargoyled. Bless me father, for I have seen. Border controls were unusually relaxed, so that we were allowed to proceed through the narrow streets to the fair, where people dressed up in "national costume" and the usual strange rituals were played out and strange aromas lingered in the air. Both sides of the street were lined with attractive colonial style buildings with beautiful forged iron balconies on which families might assemble to greet the parade. Breakfast was exceedingly colourful. Bright sunshine and warmth all day, I could weep with relief.

But in any case there wasn't a single I: for the city contained, as well as an I that was the standard referent for the self, a fictionalised I who could be made to do anything necessary for the purpose of the narrative, and a transcendent I who could only be inferred. By day, trees shaded green benches; by night, the lamps were lit and the fountain played. By the lighthouse on a Sunday afternoon, the wind blew and men were playing cricket on the hot clay in front of the new white mosque that had been built with "oil money". Climbing the hill once again, making quite good sense of all the bits, we hoped that eventually all would come together and make some kind of a picture. Coloured lights, projections of the neon signage above the ice-cream parlour on the opposite side of the street, played on the bedroom ceiling, while the early hits of Del Shannon, Buddy Holly and the Everly Brothers made their flourishes as they slowly entered the mythic dimension. Daily encounters with buildings, which hour by hour became invisible, buildings that erased themselves even as they dizzied us with the glint of their windows. Derricks on the wharf, corroded, not in use. Dogs roamed free. Dolphins in schools and small family groups, both common and bottle-nosed, would skip through the waters way beyond the harbour, unheeding our merely human life. Elegant, wide boulevards were scarcely a feature; rather, public spaces were compressed in such a way as to give comfort to the citizens. Engines were blanketed by cloud. Esoteric musics from another continent, featuring plucked, bowed and blown instruments and the persistent, spine-chilling wail of humans, hung on the short-wave band, drifting periodically. Even now, the bay was

14

dense with shipping. Every time I stayed over, my grandfather would offer to take me for a walk down to the wharf, and sometimes, my hand in his, he would detour through the old market, where turkeys gobbled in a makeshift pen and hens and ducks lay listlessly in stacked cages, and one of the stallholders, taking a shine to me, might offer me an orange or a banana, before, finally, the water-light flooded in, and there before us would be the two ancient tenders, rusting and bobbing gently at their moorings. Everybody had grown portly in the intervening years. Everybody loves you here, they said, except those that don't. Everyone tried to avoid a tiresome Englishman in the bar. Exotic variants of familiar games were played. Flags hung from every window and embrasure. For nearly an hour, we stared over the runway at the frontier, the newly built sports stadium and the distant mountains. Free association was discouraged. From the east, the wind blew, striking the edge from a clear sky to form a great dark cloud that streamed away and blotted out the sun. Ghost workers had once been lodged in the now deserted army barracks. Great commotion one morning, as one of the monkeys, a large male, had come down into the city, scattering sparrows, and now sat on a parapet, glaring balefully at passers by while picking at a piece of tinfoil. He showed us where a balcony had been abandoned to the seagulls, which were now a protected species, the wrought iron-work encrusted with guano. Here, we're all first person plural, he said, or intimated as much. Hi, we are your friends, they all said, and sometimes your relations, and we will do anything for you if you will only understand us, and this gave me great comfort and longing, though the feelings later changed, I don't know why. Horror at the sight of a one-legged man coming up the street below, observed by me and my mother from the window of the flat; my first intimation of mortality. I felt a sense of melancholy, not just because the warmth and light had been left behind, but at the thought of not belonging, of floating free. I had attributed this to the explosion, while I was still a baby, of a barge laden with ammunition in the harbour, which had caused glass to fly, woodwork to splinter, ceilings to fall and buildings to shudder, while the sky was temporarily darkened by a great mushroom cloud of smoke. Iron and steel clanged throughout the working day, cranes shuddered, men cried warnings, coaling stages loomed overhead, great vessels were removed from the sea, buoys rang out, mud was exposed, a dirty submarine leaked at the end of a detached mole, businesses flourished and expired as the years elapsed. I stumbled through the strangely familiar streets, wanting an exit, fearing that I would come face to face with myself in a different guise. In the botanical gardens, among the old cannons, we strolled in peace. In the cathedral yard, the same blue and white picture tiles, the same palm tree, now several years older and several metres taller. In the museum were fragments of neolithic and bronze age pots, Greek pots (one with a fat hairy man doing an ungainly dance on it), sarcophagi, the cargo of wrecked ships, models and miniature masks of theatrical characters. In the triumphal last room of the museum, a complete scale model of the city in which we actually stood, plus its environs and borders (the paradoxes entailed by this). In the remote distance a railway, of broad gauge, the rusted iron rails reaching beyond the distance, trembling in anticipation of a freight train from the forest. In this city, there were endless possibilities of bad faith, and to select none of them was to push one's luck. In those days a horse racing course occupied the central area of flat ground. It had once been a small, fan-shaped city completely enclosed by thick stone walls and built on three distinct levels, following natural contours. It was the end of voyaging, some said, and the entrance to Hades. It was the forlorn hope that I could bring the lost part of my life into renewed focus that kept me following the narrative whichever way it might lead. It was to be my father's final resting place. Keys played a crucial if obscure role in this narrative. Language was the only subject that was never spoken about by the citizens. Many of them were Genoese traders escaping from Napoleon, British soldiers and sailors, Jews whose ancestors had been driven from their homeland, Maltese merchants, Minorcans and French royalists. Men from the electricity station were playing dominoes in the bar. Military aircraft flew overhead. My father's ashes in a plastic box, carried as hand luggage. My grandmother used to lower a basket on a string from her apartment window, to be loaded with bread or other goods by an itinerant tradesman. My mother fell off her bicycle at the racecourse, injured her leg, and was punished for this. My uncle conducted the orchestra in a great, gloomy cave illuminated by coloured lights. Narrow passages with steps cut their way between buildings, and I recalled narrow streets where geraniums were beginning to wilt and the scent of horse droppings still lingered; a mule waiting patiently, tethered to its cart, but with an enormous erection;

shops shuttered for the holy days and feast days; the novelty and excitement of football on television in blizzardy monochrome; longing for the beach white-out. On Sundays, after we'd walked in the gardens among the tall pines and dragon trees, we would meet my uncle for lunch down by the marina – he was slow and distant as he stopped by our table. On the beach, only the encroaching shadow of the great rock towards the waning of the afternoon gave any clue that time would not continue to stand still. Once, a magnificent ur-city had been built within the confines of the present city, containing mosques and palaces; and elaborate water channels had been constructed to provide a natural water supply for the habitations and the numerous gardens below. Origin this is not; for discontinuity is a feature. Overlooking the lagoon was the "jungle", about which the less said the better. People talked freely in the streets about what was happening. Persistent, damp mist hid the family names that my father was destined to join. Portliness was a quality shared by the school chums who turned up to the afternoon event. Reclaimed land provided the location, the sea having given up its mystery to quotidian human affairs. Resemble nobody, I had tried to tell myself; but that wouldn't work here. Resisting the imperative to use the city as metaphor, an opportunity offering too perfect a fit between "proper" and "figurative" meaning, leaving no space to wander, sailors, arm in arm, wove a complex path up the main street as they returned to their ships, roaring in rough harmony. Salt was removed from the sea. Seas were frightening to all city folk when they asserted their terrible dignity. Shaping took place inside as well as outside. Shining and sweet smelling in the bright, warm sunlight lay our most lovely decoration: thousands upon thousands of white narcissi. Six great piers, standing in their own solid shadow, framed the sluice-gates. Slow, rhythmic sound of breathing of thirty thousand inhabitants. So we bought rolls, sat by the pool, swam, slept. Soldiers marched, stood at attention, men came in on bicycles, cultures jigsawed, languages melted, fused or self-destructed, women came in on foot and left by bus, economies mutated, flags fluttered or went down. Some nervous folk dived into their cars and drove at full speed to the border. Somehow, and for no reason that I can easily explain, I had left this city many years ago, and now came back as a ghost (guest). Streets and passageways became an "archipelagic zigzag". Surfaces were plastered over with a smooth layer of mortar and finished with a thin wash of exceedingly hard but finer plaster. Terrible presence dwelt in these streets, never to be recognised. The building had been undergoing recent refurbishment, as evidenced by ladders and neat piles of aggregate and brick, but in other respects was still the building in my dream. The entrance was exactly as gloomy, the tiling intact, as I remembered it from my dream and from my memory. The faces of the tower were scarred with the wounds of many bombardments. The narrow main street began to fill with excited people, and then distantly we heard the first faint strains of the approaching military band. The nearby beach resort, which had been the cause of much eager anticipation, proved to be sadly run-down and depressing. The resemblance became apparent to a great human corpse laid out on its back and covered with a winding sheet, its head to the north, its feet

The entrance was exactly as gloomy, the tiling intact, as I
remembered it

pointing at Africa. The sun began to shine fiercely. The town drunk marched solemnly in front of the band master, using a rolled-up newspaper, or perhaps a stick, to mimic his complicated twirls and thrusts, until he was led away gently by police. The town tramp, often observed squatting with a beer bottle in various locations throughout my childhood, was known by a single nickname, which I associated with "shit", because other children had made me look at the occasional deposit he left; but when many years later he was finally taken into hospital and died, the local newspaper report, which gave his hitherto unknown full name, seemed to be about someone else entirely. The weather was perfect for the cable car. There was no hinterland to speak of. They crept down the wall from the garden next door, clinging on suckered feet, and I now believe they were geckos, but my father used to call them salamanders. They took refuge in the cliffs above the city. This is pre-linguistic, unrepresentable memory. This narrator isn't and is in the story, or it could be my mother, I don't know, I'm tired and I want to go to sleep. This, the steepling alleyway with the centre railing, midway on my journey to school, was the place where I first heard Lorca's voice; and where a girl from the high school, whom I'd observed with longing for days, stopped me to ask me my name, and I was unable to answer. To reinvent this space would pose a terrifying problem. Traders would arrive every day, it was recalled, crossing the frontier (the point at which cobbles gave way to tarmac); one wore a flat hat, on which he balanced his comestibles as he slow-marched proudly around the city, proclaiming; another hauled a wagon laden with water-barrels; and a herd of

This, the steepling alleyway with the centre railing.

goats preceded a third, who would stop as required to milk one for the convenience of a customer, unless I have this wrong. Two tribes inhabited the city, each of a separate persuasion; but chance alone determined which of the two any individual citizen might fall under, and so it was impossible to be certain of avoiding offence. "Uncle Arthur" was a common name for a single man living in the apartment upstairs, possibly homosexual or possibly not, though this was not a subject for debate, who might have a room dedicated entirely to an aviary of finches, or else would possess a gramophone capable of putting out stereophonic sound, years before such a novelty became commonplace. Unsure of what I was doing, I carried the casket to its resting place. Unwittingly, we were stepping on an ancient sea-bed. Up by the long abandoned military battery, swirling in cloud, the gulls screamed in panic as a griffon vulture glided past, the bolder among them harrying the big dark bird from their skies. Voices were placed at precise locations, and, to our amazement, a military band marched slowly and purposefully from the left-hand speaker to the right. Walking back to the Continental Hotel, we talked about what had been lost and gained. We heard about the bombs. We heard, but did not see, the fireworks. We used to play in the ruins of what had once been the Grand Stores, bombed during "the war". We went to a gate in the side of the rock, which when unlocked revealed a long, narrow passage, at the end of which was a trapdoor let into the floor, and one by one we descended a flight of wooden steps about twelve feet long, at the bottom of which we saw a large hall or cave that resembled somewhat a huge rabbit warren; its floor appeared to be very wet and the light illuminating it made it look very dangerous to walk on, but to my surprise it was quite easy to move about and not near so dangerous as it first seemed; and so after passing through this cave we descended slightly, rounding a bend in so doing, where we were told that here it would be necessary for us to slide down a knotted rope about eight feet long, which required effort but which we managed quite well; and once again gaining a foothold we found we were standing in another cave or hall, the walls of which looked as if they had been carved by some primitive sculptor, some of the carvings resembling faces, some flowers and foliage, and I looked round for a second exit but there seemed to be none. We were led by an Irish Christian Brother round another bend, necessitating a crawl on our hands and knees through a small gap between two rocks, coming out on a high rock and between this and a rock on the other side where it was necessary for us to cross, some kind engineer had fixed and fastened a rope, so in single file we passed hand over hand along this rope to the other side, taking a foothold whenever and wherever possible, till we reached another large cave, the most beautiful we had so far seen, with objects like pipes and icicles in white, cream, grey and brownish-red, and there were other objects that resembled elephants' ears, and clusters of pipe-like objects close together which when tapped gave all different sounds; and there were other creations of nature that resembled very closely a pulpit, spears and knives and many other weird instruments, but there were also occasional pools of water which were said to be very deep and dangerous if one had the ill luck to fall into one, and in every dark spot everything seemed so deathly quiet that it seemed there was no coming back from this. When television was first introduced, I became frightened at the first strains of the music for "The Invisible Man", even though (or especially because) a storm of interference scarcely permitted any clear view of the protagonist as he removed his bandages to reveal his nothingness. When the plane landed at the airport late Thursday afternoon I felt an unexpected welling of emotion. Why I left in the first place is because I wanted to blur the distinction between objects that were situated in space and those that were not. Wild birds passed this way. With regard to my return, it appears to be a case of denying my presence in the act of affirming it. Years later, I was to write a poem called "El Hombre Invisible", which tried to locate that fear. You could say I'm trying to get to the point where I'm able to begin.

2 City Break

ACROSS THE river and via the island lots of people milling around watching street performances a blues band a weird mime show which reminded you of the lodger and his Japanese girlfriend and there they were being exceptionally good monkeys in front of a seemingly appreciative crowd then at the top there was a terrific view the gentle swell of the river a scary glass of wine a detour through the space-age hall where two models were laughing and being photographed and now the sun had almost set leaving behind a beautiful pink and mauve sky the buskers and more street performers body poets creatures eating fire and a jazz band a man in tails irritating people with takeaway food you forgot to mention the woman with the haunting voice and the bells on her calf who sang about the distant mountains in front of a statue amid disasters and other fun like this the station the liberation monument the menagerie you wanted to kidnap a baby lion with enormous paws all of which interfered with the schedule the bank was closed so you had to go to the garden and drink and eat and put yourself in a better mood but a queue had formed and they wouldn't reopen the bank because they couldn't find the keys and not only that the train reservation computer had broken down and anyway the international tickets happened somewhere else so cheques could only be cashed in a funny bank where the customers took the ladies behind the counter out for coffee and then everything became very late the metro station the river again the bank was still shut but the reservation machine was working again but you collapsed into a bus before suppertime found the Irish pub which was much like all Irish pubs in all the cities of the world having little Irish about it apart from serving Guinness and had to play games in trying circumstances accompanied by three chattering nuns who didn't seem very pleased to see you and were standing outside in the passage waiting a bit of a contrast it took seven and a half hours checking into the hotel a tiny dark room and a shower down the corridor hunting for food with anxiety about money and time spilling brandy on the carpet impossible it's impossible to continue it's the last straw an invasion by two young men in addition to the nuns frenetic shopping your dreams were realised in a wonderful blue and silver train as dusk fell again a little Down's syndrome girl insisted on giving you many kisses quite impossible and finally a bit of a letdown a big wooden bed much recovery and unpacking taking to the streets the heat making an interesting circular walk including the cathedral beautiful though slightly seedier than the photos had led you to believe the royal palace guarded by bus-conductors with machine guns a beautifully fitted together set of buildings in the bright sunshine that faded to haze the square the irregular façades on which pigeons perched the majesty of the Renaissance some unidentified "sights" an unsuccessful diversion very hot into the palisaded and pedestrianised zones containing all the fashionable boutiques where you re-emerged into the street it was dark but quite hectic nowadays there is a large immigrant population attached but not attached kind of opposite and free-floating on the river-bank two young men in leather jackets fishing with their dog an oily scum under the steel bridge the soup was itself followed by another soup course which was a big mistake and due to another error an over-large egg salad to finish this was not the restaurant you had been recommended where you would have expected grilled pike-perch fillet with a small dollop of raspberry sauce Thai steamed rice and pineapple and where your companion could have had red mullet fillets with basil sauce no that was a different one it had a website or perhaps that was in a different city there was a canary singing just near the room in a cage on a window ledge very upset the episode of the lion cub may have occurred at this point the station again the metro steaming hot a bullet without air-conditioning overcrowded until people changed seats confusing the ticket inspector a lady in a green dress a large monument on a hill which was the geographical centre the building was public and gloomy yellow flattish and with hardly any signs of life the organs bronze the ground grey and purple night

Some unidentified "sights".

fell on the terrace all chattering with great excitement a new bench on cobblestones you shouting in your dreams a lawn of curiously fleshy grass bordered by beds of roses shrubs evergreen trees and strange succulent type plants and many other plants in pots and vines trailed over the top though the geraniums had stopped flowering a grey cat called Lucy many flies and ants there was a swimming pool in the shade of the terrace where you sat while people appeared and disappeared in the endless process of preparing for departure disappearing completely at last a replica of the BBC World Service hanging in the air running and conscious cars and bikes rushing up the road hurried coffee sun brightening the sky a never-ending amount of traffic nobody stopped and it soon became clear it was too late bridges crammed full of people by balancing on flowerpots you could see over their heads but you gave up after a while and walked around the adjoining church grounds where there was a spectacular if misty view through a coin-in-the-slot telescope the winding streets a long march would be forthcoming but sadly it was completely unsuccessful having covered the central area two or three times in the process watching all the preparations in the sanctuary the bus the long conversations with people who wanted to find out what you thought of "the world" and what you had been and what you had done and what you would be doing with your life and then once more to the bank and to the post office a delightful recreation of the Franciscan monastery that had once stood on the site but to your surprise it was closed somebody said there were regional elections all the little people on little wooden beds packed together and shops and restaurants selling hamburgers only too late spotting a plate of mixed fish which had everything you'd ever wanted on it whereupon cloud and humidity gave way to sunshine two cats on a flat roof so you hung around until the supermarket opened bought some miniature bottles and went back to the station a young man with a naked stump for one leg and crutches laid by slumped motionless in the subway next to a small polystyrene container with a few coins in it rows of gypsies holding out embroidered rugs and shawls for sale set off once again just missed the bus in the bar were sailors from the Spanish Armada watching football on TV you could do this now cloud descended the sky repeatedly darkened and yellowed part of the road was missing and this caused the bus some delay a very nice promenade behind the hotel coffee and Coke and big juicy raisins most places were closed but were much prettier at night the fountain that changed colours purple and pink and found a dressing gown in blue silk with embroidered flowers to walk down in it the pitch blackness just inside drunk with 12° pilsner beer at 11.30 pm in the hotel over which Venus shines next to the moon as Leonard Cohen's "Suzanne" plays on the radio a choice of films either *Emmanuelle, die Nackte von Sados* or *Pussy in the Bathhouse* walk all the way till morning each morning the church-bells chime without melody or rhythm little sweet biscuits plain toast didn't sleep very well for mopeds screaming down the alleyway streetcleaners and loud altercations what a chore going on and on without paradigm shift all the way to change some money fail to make contact whether to or not whether to meet tonight or not whether or not you phoned the

hotel but failed bought provisions and little brown
bowls which were your treasure but did not get brandy
all this took three hours organising and pottering making you hot and bothered had seen the sunrise the station cafeteria the shop (closed) thought a suitcase was
a bomb bought magazines went through narrow foot-
paths with tiny people on them a bag belonging to a
fat man with a fat cigar fell on the woman next to him
air-conditioning cold hit all your carefully laid plans a
bar round the corner just closing for the night a long
walk then to the celebrated art gallery with one of the
most important collections in the region where imagination's purely wrecked and everything is remarkable
and back again a fountain again a statue of a lady being
pulled along by lions beautiful wide avenues soft and
wooded and the houses all changed their style to rough
multi-grey stone with muted roofs all the clever money
had moved here confronted with millions of noisy
people and nobody to help queued for some money
then along the avenue with all the smart shops but
couldn't go any further because the workers were on
strike feeling decidedly sore needed some wine joined
an enormous queue outside an ice-cream shop to com-
pensate and you could see the very cannonballs
embedded in the walls in and around the ramparts in
the cathedral and out to the old town you have to see
the old town but first there's early 20th century architecture including a cubist lamp-post neo-renaissance
and art nouveau buildings and an example of early
modernism severe plate-glass all the way round but
beyond the runes of power the municipal piles the balcony from where the crowds were greeted in those terrible days but you can't leave the city without a visit to

the old town terribly cramped and quaint the walls crumbling subject to restoration donations gratefully received the celebrated "mediaeval core" a community known to have existed here since the Bronze and Iron ages and the Jewish quarter a labyrinth of alleyways and such but there are no Jews any more not since the great charter and the wool merchants passed through here time running out there haven't been any for some time an epoch even the Jewish quarter without Jews or the Arab quarter no Arabs they have all been banished to the "outlying districts" and you peered into the cemetery from the gate near the bridge below the other bridge near the national theatre (a "Mecca for culture lovers") the poor people names carved from memory were rounded up here were walled in were driven out were slaughtered in their hundreds and thousands the terrible days terrible years glass shattered blood in the runnels breasts hacked off eviscerations performed in the classical fashion by the approved method children terrified belongings scattered names misplaced businesses ransacked all tidied up now names and bones and names and bones and artefacts with little labels to remember them by little labels arranged methodically in the museum in the old town so quaint with the evocative street names the street of the revolution the winding stair of tears the avenue of despair boulevard of dreadful transgression square of hideous metastasis and gloom the old cemetery yes you must see the old cemetery and here you are this is the place this must be the place to which all data trails tend the place where all income streams flow here you are the very place a famous composer is here and you are here at the end of all narratives the place

You peered into the cemetery from the gate near the bridge.

sanctified by history upon which still stands the old
opera house definitely worth a visit meet your friends
there for a coffee as people used to do in the old days
but nobody showed up so you had to get out of here
there's nowhere to go you consulted the map so conve-
niently provided by the tourist board in association
with the chamber of commerce here's Konrad Ade-
nauer street there's Winston Churchill boulevard and
General Charles de Gaulle place which is not called
that any more but in any case none of this was marked
on the map not at any rate the place from where you
headed for the hills after lunch in a restaurant where
the menu was completely incomprehensible soon after
which you found yourself at the periphery the city lim-
its the ring road or peripheral highway where the traffic fled flashing by on the overpass pedestrians this
way on the underpass there was a drive-in or drive-
through where you were so nearly assailed by two dogs
one of them a giant very nearly left your bag behind
on a miserable journey through the underpass and
therefore under the overpass which was a boulevard
that had been driven through the amazing labyrinth
and beyond hot and stuffy bumpy with poor street
lighting in that world outside beyond the periphery the
old suburbs the outskirts the "outlying districts" where
the riot police patrol as dusk falls protecting the centre
in their vehicles dilapidated furniture on the street dis-
tressed concrete drainage sumps inscrutable graffiti
none of this shown on the map very probably recent
developments usual scatter of tower blocks railway
lines flat wagons bearing armoured personnel carriers
patches of greenery giving way to gravel warehouses
the celebrated powder mill had evidently vanished too

The street of the revolution the winding stair of tears the
avenue of despair boulevard of dreadful transgression.

and now pylons and stadiums terribly wet and glistening platforms placards hoardings a distant vista of supermarkets and hypermarkets in the even more distant Eurozone the new citadel of commerce since the millennium soon to be connected on all sides reached by floodlit ribbon development chain-link fencing cycle tracks storm drains all within the larger metropolitan area where programmes of cultural activity are promised but it is your "delight to set out towards a horizon"….

3 City of Grain Elevators

HOW BEAUTIFUL the distant, wispy clouds were in an otherwise clear cerulean sky. Early Sunday morning, and little traffic on the roads. The bag had begun to split at the sides. Coffee was taken, one capuccino and one filter, and a Danish pastry shared. Perpendicular architecture. Waiting to be called. The various aircraft moved slowly into and out of their positions at the boarding gates. In a field that raced by, chickens ran to be fed. A book had been forgotten – fortunately, little damage was done. The feeling, once all the arrangements had been made and the requirements of safety and bureaucracy complied with, that matters were out of their hands and that therefore there was no alternative but to sit back and let events take their course – and the comfort in this. Water in a glass, the small ice cubes swiftly disappearing. Shoes were removed.

Hunger. The slow movement of metal in wind. On an impulse, they took a taxi, possible outcomes having become evident. These things would live on in their memories, or if not in their memories then in the record, on paper or laptop computer, as an aid to or substitute for memory. Whether in fact a city existed was as yet unknown – the photographs had been removed.

THE GREEN of the suburbs took them by surprise. They were driven along the side of the cemetery for some minutes, then turned into a tree-lined avenue. The woman with the key was not at home. Houses of every design, colour and size lined the avenue; some sported notices in their porches inviting blessings on the nation. There was a choice of beer. A table wobbled. Some time later, they were admitted to the place they had imagined, which was somewhat bigger than they had anticipated. At 3am, distant birdsong was heard, its repetitive nature leading to the suggestion that it was produced in captivity. Clanging of a hammer echoed in the avenue. The rain came down; it looked as though it would settle for the day. They would never forget this. A magnifying glass and some coasters on a low table. The length of the corridor surprised and delighted them. Voile veiled the windows. Chilled white wine was poured. Books, postcards and other items were propped on the ledge of the wood panelling that ran all the way round the room. In half the attic, chairs had been drawn up, as though for an event that would never now happen. Cleaning fluids of all kinds produced milky stains in the black lacquer.

The length of the corridor surprised and delighted them.

Dumpsters were positioned next door. The same black youth, his head tightly bandaged, racing endlessly up and down the escalator in the subway station, from morning until late afternoon. Another branch in the path. Slipping on mud, twice. Unseasonable rain, and an absence of population. Flimsy rain jackets were hurriedly unrolled, but they produced more moisture inside than they repelled outside. Evidence of wealth, but none of its production. Wings were invented here. The way the suicide of the defence ministry adviser was reported was interesting. They would always remember how footsore they were. A purple house, and the picture in a newspaper of a purple polar bear, its colour the inadvertent side-effect of medication. Flags.

ON MONDAY morning, senior citizens sheltering from the rain played cards in a coffee-shop. When the lights indicated, they crossed the road behind the old lady, but on the other side she made to turn right while they turned left; confusion ensued, resolved with smiles and polite formulations. Several of the houses appeared to be uninhabited, or offered for sale or rent; others may have been left empty by their inhabitants for the summer season. It was uncertain which was the correct way in. The new owner indicated that he intended to pay an official visit on Tuesday. But that was when he was naïve and lacking in experience. The kettle whistled, and would not yield. The time and the ambient temperature were projected. As daylight approached , it faded and was finally invisible. "I can't think of a wine shop, but there is a liquor store three blocks away where you can get wine." Sandwiches and soft drinks were consumed. Shoes were examined, including the soles. In the art gallery, giggling housewives and silent teenagers were shepherded quickly past the modern art. Flash photography was not permitted. The road led undeviatingly through neighbourhoods of different ethnicities, social classes and economic brackets. Once again, the clouds came over and it turned humid. A sofas-on-the-street kind of neighbourhood. Italian delicacies and fresh produce were offered for sale. After some discussion, a box of bin-liners was produced. The outline, against a grey sky, of the psychiatric institution, extensive and grim as a castle. A glimpse of the park and lake, impossibly enticing. Inside the apartment, John Coltrane played "My Favorite Things"; outside, the builders shouted at one another. Three pear-shaped wax candles in the disused fireplace: one milky yellow, one raspberry coloured, the third lime green. The phone rang four times, the answering machine was triggered, but after a series of clicks and whirrs no message was left. After several years, the memories would still be strong, if inevitably selective.

WHAT HAD once been a show tune was transformed into something hinting at eastern modes, full of melancholy and yearning. The big blue refuse truck moved slowly up the residential street. Its roar receded slowly, until eventually it was heard no more. Evidence of the length of time since the last inhabitants left: the calendar's leaves torn off only up to May 7. You could say they got their fingers burnt. Distant siren. Rubble and a rectangular trench in the back yard – the back of

Inside the apartment, John Coltrane played "My Favorite Things"; outside, the builders shouted at one another.

the house, which would otherwise have been exposed, temporarily covered with plywood boarding, the only evidence of the builders who had worked through the evening in a thunderstorm. "The news" was presented in a way that brooked no argument. Presently, the sky cleared, and the streets, vast runnels only an hour previously, were dry once more. Information was presented as entertainment, and vice versa. An ambulance charged. It was terrifying in its symmetry. Rye bread, ham and salami were unpacked. Books were consumed. A clockwork monster and a furry hedgehog on top of a clock. Swarms of sparrows, boldly pecking. Although there was a candle in every window, there was very little information outside the building. Part of the mound of rubble had been sheared off by the force of the rain during the night, leaving an unstable cliff edge, and had fallen into the trench – the remainder of which had filled with milky water. The smell of coffee, the quiet sound of the rain. A china rabbit on a small chest. The further they went downtown, the more bizarre the architecture appeared. A man with bare arms and a snake round his neck inquired how they were doing. Japanese lamps, kites, leather belts, T-shirts and novelty crockery were offered for sale. Wandering in ever increasing circles, coming across the same streets again and again. A franchise corner store, limited and high-priced – that was where you got the phone cards. A breakfast wrap was ordered. Breeze-blocks were delivered. The waitress was extremely friendly, but then disappeared for half an hour. Passing the outdoor tables of the bar, the man suddenly turned and barked, "You know, alcohol is a *drug*!" then continued calmly on his way. Thousands of gravestones in the sunshine. Golfers had taken over the entire space. A man examining a blue wheelie bin at the verge turned round and smiled: "I'm going through my own garbage!" A burly man led two huge black dogs that walked as he jogged. The animals, visible between the slats, moved only minimally – all visitors having departed. This would live on in their imagination for a long time, or if not in their imagination at least in their memory. From the number of people congregated on benches round the tennis courts, it was clear this was serious stuff. Ice cream was not available because the ice cream machine was frozen. The girl was leafing through what could have been a poetry magazine or a book of recipes; her companion was reading *Moby-Dick*.

THE WEATHER front moved on, and the day cleared. It became so much more interesting. Budget cuts were discussed. A hummus wrap or a breakfast wrap? One species had the curiosity to want to make a spectacle of all the others, and the intelligence to be able to round them up and keep them in the one place in order to do so. They were sitting around disconsolately; it wasn't unreasonable. It was a major source of buzz. The gorillas spent most of their time avoiding the gaze of the humans who had come to view them. The bison moved slightly in the sun. "That's half-pig, half-monkey" was one remark. Glittering water at the edge of the promenade. Extremely slow food. Bubbles of cloud welled ominously at the horizon, but it seemed the weather front was receding again. She wore blond dreadlocks tucked into a voluminous woollen hat. Bungalows lined the edge of pleasant woodland. The bandanna came off. It was the second time in two days, at exactly the same spot, that someone had called from a passing car, asking for directions that they could not provide. There was too much of a frantic quality, you got edgy here. A couple had appeared to quit their café table, but returned quickly to reclaim it. "Your mother never liked Herbie's mother," said the woman. Whole cakes were displayed under glass. As evening came on, people started to bring their own chairs for an open-air gathering. A sudden influx of about a hundred young cyclists riding up the avenue. The night had been the warmest yet, and even the sheet felt oppressive. A tiny caterpillar truck backed into the alley delivering its pallet. Timber planks were brought; they were to be used for the framework. They looked as though they were moving house by bus. Everything was used up before appearing again in different guises. The woman uttered a piercing shriek from the back of the bus, but the man at the front went on patiently searching through his pockets for change with which to pay the driver. Ice creams were worth two tickets, but you had to walk a block for the tickets. First a drum, then a bass guitar, then a whole band, but the audience hadn't even turned up yet. Sharp winds blew in from the lake, and napkins and paper cups were scattered. To their left, the golden dome and the clock they had surveyed so often, recorded by the webcam on the website, was revealed in "real life". It was designated a national historic landmark in 1986. To make it safer and more aesthetically pleasing, the entire deck and support systems had been replaced. They needed to watch their food, lest the birds help themselves. The prognosis was mixed. Birds of paradise appeared over the "vast reaches of his domain". Down the stairs to the cellar, the place of cleansing and therefore of fear. The possibilities of trips up tall buildings, round lakes and into entirely other regions were idly discussed. Two bridges, and getting them mixed up. The voice of a radio celebrity on your answering machine, offered as a prize. The only guided missile cruiser open to the public. Shearing bricks in two on a Sunday morning. It was a liquidity event that validated the moment. They were laying the foundations. Long notes were initiated. They had built a considerable extent of wall. She appeared at just the wrong moment, that of the arrival of the owner. Both machines worked perfectly well, in fact the phrase "like a dream" came to mind. Ambient temperatures were all over the place. Ants in the pantry were disposed of. Hot and bone dry at last. He dreamt that he was locked out of his computer, having deliberately committed a violation. They were to talk about it for days, and even years, ahead. Jewels and clams were offered for sale. The barman, on hearing where he was from, shook his hand effusively, and a woman customer at the bar wondered aloud why he'd chosen to come here. The walk wasn't worth the outcome. Lights came on in the passageway.

AT THE end of the ornamental lake, a faint aroma of sewage. It was glorious to watch the swallows skimming low over the lake and the surrounding grassy banks. A vast range of sandwiches was listed, though upon closer inspection they all seemed virtually identical. The lake, olive with light blue rippling highlights as the sun came out. Brightly coloured banners hanging between the Ionian columns. Boys sketching on the promenade. She rummaged in the bag for her dark glasses. A sandwich fit for a king *and* a queen. The potato chips tasted particularly lovely. A distant view of trucks moving on the highway past the historical museum. As each jogger approached, they had to make a decision whether to acknowledge them or not. A black pug had done its business. The sky seemed to drain colour from the park and the surrounding buildings whenever the sun went in. Yellow was the colour of the bus. A shopping district in hell. Tattoo parlours abounded. Many of the shops were for sale or rent. The area beneath the railway bridge was plentifully supplied with guano. They were beginning to figure out how the parkways intersected with the system of avenues and streets, but even so it was still a mild shock to come out from a new angle at the familiar corner with the bookshop and café. A baby rabbit emerged from under a parked car. It led its owner back home. Hot air from the tropics was met by a cold front moving in from the lakes. A sparrow dipped its beak in a stainless steel bowl of water on the pavement. A little girl lay with her head on one dog and her feet on another. The melancholy of the jazz singer on late night radio, negotiating the angles and by-ways of a melody that sounded as though it had been abandoned on the farthest coast.

THEY FELT obliged to participate in the practices of visitors, although really they would have preferred their usual routines. The arrangements in the bus station, remembered from over 25 years ago. A huge slam on the back of the bus from a surly would-be passenger. Photographing the statue of a founder of the nation in the main square. The bus driver was an elderly woman in sunglasses; it was clearly her first time driving a bus on this route; once, she went astray at an intersection, ending up on the freeway and having to be guided back onto the regular route by one of the passengers, and later she drove over deep ruts, causing the vehicle almost to shake apart. The tallest building lorded it over the rest. A flag flew at half-mast; possibly because a favourite comedian had died the day before. Mist in the distance shrouded part of a science fiction skyline. Another country lay opposite, but with familiar furniture. The spray came off the fall in concentric clouds. Industrial tubes and domes, rust and disused railway tracks: such were the first impressions on crossing the bridge. Mildew in the marina; gas cylinders; container trucks in a vast parking lot. At least one other person had a map. Pylons strode across the estuary, the great cables dipping above the waves. They were entering a deaf child area. Purple and yellow flowers on the waste ground of an island between cities. Suddenly, the neighbourhood changed. A squirrel skittered across a red roof. Dogs nosed their grocery bags. Local people showed pride in their neighbourhood. The band consisted of Senegalese, African-Americans and Americans. A woman's voice that had previously been heard on an answering machine was now aired on the radio. She was told she looked like Paul McCartney. A hat signified African origins, but most of the audience was white. Beer was not available for taking out. Motorised pedal scooters, very noisy, were ridden on the sidewalk with impunity. A boy repeatedly leapt to try and touch the road sign. Running while clutching weights; running while clutching a bottle of water; running while clutching nothing. Floating scum. A jet airliner flying below the clouds. In the distance, classical statuary; the museum; the pedestrians' and cyclists' bridge. Sparrows were abundant in every location. A wheelie bin was chained to a lamp-post. The workmen hacked away relentlessly at the roof tiles from morning till late afternoon; the following day a man, perhaps the owner, appeared on the balcony to contemplate the result. A resident of the 100 block of O__ reports an unknown black man, 5'8" all dressed in black, who did enter the residence and did steal 3 credit cards. The thrice attempted delivery of a computer was documented by stickers affixed to the door. Two men in beards, dark glasses, khaki shorts, sandals, each carrying a guitar case. The college clock struck the quarter-hour. Odd to see a white man in one of those gaudily coloured loose suits with half-mast pants and matching hat. A thick-spectacled black man with a grizzled beard, in shorts, bare-chested, wheeled his bicycle up to the bin, parked it, opened the bin to inspect the contents, removed a transparent plastic glove from his bicycle bag, put it on one hand, leant into the bin propelling his feet off the ground and, reaching within, withdrew a bottle which he first placed on the ground, then, after closing the lid, removed it to the bicycle bag and moved on to the next bin – talking to himself the whole while. A fluorescent yellow tennis ball was thrown into the lake for the black retriever to fetch, concentric ripples widening from the plunge of its heavy form. Water, here calm, was elsewhere impelled by titanic forces in opposition, such that they cancelled each other, and thus produced the semblance of calm. They remembered the distant cloud in front of the distant buildings that turned out to be vapour from the falls. She often felt nostalgia for an experience even before it had ended. A famous architect had designed the house on the corner, described as "like a boat", though length was possibly the only resemblance. Large ants occasionally wandered into the apartment and circled aimlessly until either they somehow found their way out or were exterminated. Cool haze came as a balm and contrast to the hot sunshine of the previous two days. A model of the city when it was a village – rather dusty. At the side of the church, the Loaves & Fishes Restaurant. Silent attendants staffed the Great Wall Chinese restaurant. They bought ice creams in glasses one could take home. Courteously, the cyclist pinged his bell as he came up behind, and thanked them for making way as he rode past. A Japanese garden tucked into the curve of the ring-road. Grey-white was the colour of the sky – the sun a brighter white patch in it. A grand piano with electric lamps built in, when that was the latest technology. Cars converted into works of art and mounted at various points in the city. Small children were wheeled round in brightly painted four-wheel hand trolleys. They read the story of how the city had been burned to the ground even before it was born, and of its rise to power within 50 years, and its subsequent industrial decline in the last half of the 20th century. They agreed they would never forget this.

The metaphysical abyss, filled by work.

THE RADIO station was hard to find, in either sense. It was now too hot to work. She had had to learn all the new technology at once. They were supposed to be looking for a building fronted by a parking lot; but parking lots fronted all the buildings. They searched for another copy of the book that had been left in the toilet. Symmetry underlay the design of the railings. Styrofoam cups were offered, to be filled with water ad lib. They heard a fly buzz in the recording studio. All the trains were inbound, meaning the outbound limit had been reached. The building felt like a school, and was a school. A resident reports, while at the foot of F__ at 5. 20am she sat in a friend's vehicle with a His- panic male called "Aida" or "Chico", 5'3" medium build with a buzz cut and hoop earring in the left ear. Railway lines had once ringed the city, but all were gone now. Pot luck was expected on Sunday. The rea- son many of the houses were divided in two was eco- nomics, as the model showed. The way vowel and con- sonant sounds could interfere with the timbre. They had not even entered the municipal building, and that the lighting in the corridor could be fixed at all was a major surprise. In the early hours of the morning there was a spat outside the house between a swearing man (or woman) and an unknown opponent – with unknown result. The foundation blocks had finally been laid, and the site filled in with dirt. The noise of the digger was quite insupportable. The dewpoint tem- perature just went up and up. Pushing as hard as possi- ble and for as long as possible in a particular direction appeared to be the best way to achieve a result. If the window was open, the flute could not be heard above the din from the building site; but if the window was closed, it became too hot unless the fan was switched on – again rendering the flute inaudible. Notebooks were filled, one after another. Her interview technique was gentle, and elicited the right result. Water had left their bodies copiously during the night. The waiters were probably students at the city's university on their vacation jobs; at any rate, the service was eager but erratic. All quiet on the bookstore front. The houses in the avenue simply refused to be photographed. A second visit brought everything into much clearer focus. High-priced and very fragile. The waiter said he had been made to sleep in a room above the restaurant – it wasn't clear if he was joking. They decided that if they were still feeling guilty by Monday morning there was still time to do something about it. A spot of detective work, and contact was made. As the weeks wore on, the same people could be recognised walking up and down the avenue or patronising the numerous bars and restaurants that lined it. An arrangement in cast iron, ceramic and wood. Architecture was always more attractive when it was lived in. Wooden flutes were very cheap. Singing was heard from the bathroom. The metaphysical abyss, filled by work. Two muffins, some milk and the paper. Customs of another city, another country, maintained here for comfort. A schedule was thrown out of kilter by the change in the weather. Clamminess reached far beyond the confines of the city. The pain in their ankles throughout the night would always live on as a memory. "Will you switch off the air?" asked a woman in the shop. Wing glasses made her look like a madwoman. The windscreen had suffered an extensive crack and looked as though it might shatter at any moment. They headed north, far

Deer had repeatedly stripped the branches, so that they had
been permanently laid bare and the tree was killed.

beyond the boundaries they had already explored. Everybody brought a contribution. Furniture was built out of scrap steel, or was inflatable. There was always another T-shirt to be bought. They had repeatedly been told that the way they talked was lovable, but the effect produced was that of alienation. Food and drink was offered from all directions. The evening darkened over the gathering on the balcony. Nothing was certain: what the next job would be, where they would be living, who their friends would be. A disavowal of content did not bear much close examination. Gravel had been shovelled into the extension: that was new.

ELSEWHERE, MEANWHILE, the war continued unabated.

THE GLUTINOUS scent of a breakfast cereal hung over the plant. An extremely rusty building appeared. A cruise ship, out of condition, or commission. They were taken south of the city, where deer, rabbits, wild turkey, herons, hawks (engaged in mid-air courtship), nuthatches, chickadees, frogs, snakes and muskrats were observed, and once a beaver followed them briefly down the woodland path. Cool breeze from the shoreline. The print of a deer on the muddy path. The rumble of a freight train passing unseen behind the trees at the far side of the marshes. Deer had repeatedly stripped the branches, so that they had been permanently laid bare and the tree was killed. Disused grain elevators and factories amid the tracks. The sun going down behind the abandoned plants. He described how he had spent a year of his life living under canvas

The sun going down behind the abandoned plants.

14,000ft in the mountains, next to a dying cannabis farm, reading poetry and fetching his own water from a stream every day. In the woods, the closeness of the city was quickly forgotten. Beer, wings, fries, conversation and a yellow half-moon. The mysterious, decaying industrial structures at the horizon.

4 Drowned City

A CITY convinces by the form it creates, not by argument. But when its time comes, the end can be swift. Grey outlines of churches, offices, warehouses, girders, etc. Brownish, clay-like stuff was used extensively. Cold Chinese food. A black man, whimpering, had been cornered by police like an animal in the garden. Flashback. He freaked out, went on a binge, spent $25 on a "relief massage" and lost his sweatshirt. He had insisted on picking up a discarded cable drum for use as a table, which was a big mistake. He was uptight because his woman was leaving him. She spoke of voices in the wind. She said that Krishnamurti said the followers of Zen were "doomed". She asked why people liked the city, and was told "Because it's full of crazy people doing meaningless things." Four homeless social workers crowded into the office, phoning round for stopgaps. It was a huge green psycho-bubble filled with water in which people swam. For more than 250 years excavators found no human remains.

ON THE radio JC Bach followed CPE; then John Lee Hooker singing "Tupelo": the poor people, they had no place to go. Once there was order, but now there is disorder, they claimed, and the answer is faith: that is, if we believe, never mind in what, we shall be saved; this is called existentialism. Their bodies radiated like beacons. The preacher went around in sky-blue vestments, chanting or mumbling (his wife or female personal assistant in tow, singing harmony), and was once observed standing outside the hotel lobby, his hands outstretched to the sky. The radio, Coltrane, "Africa Brass", faded into the midnight air. There was incense, frying food and a ten-year-old kid playing drums. There were rows of shops, bars, houses, an amphitheatre, a small theatre, a lovely house with terracotta and black plastering patterned with fleur-de-lys like on Florentine leatherwork, and a gym, and among all these, dead bodies in various postures. They remembered the smell of cats, they recalled flea-ridden rooms, electric bar firelight bouncing off dusty Melanex wallpaper. They were in sight of land at last. Through a synthesis of A (that which remains constant) and B (feelings/emotions) we arrive at C, which is actually a departure point. Colours: muted oranges, yellows, greens, blues. Indifferent saxophone mingled with a police siren. Oily pools in the gutters. One of them was offered a joint and some strange, fruity-flavoured rosé wine. On late-night TV, Bo Diddley playing classical violin. Reconstituted rooms featured furniture, lamps, sculpture and daily implements for living, tools, cookware, plates, cups, eating utensils, cosmetics. The TV worked if you bashed it on the side. Various items of clothing, confectionery and a suitcase, a bottle of green peppermint cordial, a French phrase-book, a bar of chocolate and a candle, all waiting for an advertised festival which never happened, which would never now happen again.

THEY WERE rounded up into work camps and held by armed guards. They were prevented from leaving as the waters rose. There was an alternative. A steamer played "Bye Bye Blackbird" as it sailed away. The violence that followed the floods helped persuade many to move north. And when they did decide to leave, they took people with them that otherwise had no means of getting out of the city, even though they were piled on top of each other in the van and they had to drill holes in abandoned cars' gas tanks to get enough fuel to leave. "All our people had evacuated and we locked the city down," said the chief of police. Before they were close enough to speak, they began firing their weapons over the group's heads. But even as they were closing the bridge, the authorities were telling people that it was the only way out of the city. In addition to security concerns, an unmoored vessel on the river raised the threat level. It was not a question of if but when. It was only a matter of time. Police from surrounding jurisdictions shut down several access points to one of the only ways out, effectively trapping victims in the devastated city. The bridge was the major artery heading west. The city would have been overwhelmed by the influx, it was said. These were code words.

AROUND NOON, the military finally reached the convention centre and began feeding people. While the mood at the centre improved, many people didn't want to eat. A man screamed at a woman to look at the body of a person who died while waiting for buses to rescue them. Dozens of old people, obviously from a nursing home, were dumped in the middle of the street and were dying in the blistering sun. Couple that with the fact that it was very hot, there was dirty water and mosquitoes everywhere. Every day they would say the buses were coming, but they didn't come, everything was sitting in that house and slowly drowning, it now began to pour down rain, but it didn't dampen their enthusiasm, for, miraculously, they had internet, though no phones, no electricity, and no running water, and the future was murky, but, one of them said, my son will now witness it, the same rebuilding I did as a child, as a child enjoys sitting in the park across from the convention centre, likes to feel the sun on her face and escape the frigid air inside the temporary shelter. With two other people, he was set adrift on a raft. Water snakes coiled themselves among the crushed palisades. While the ground seemed to be swaying all morning, he felt weak and thought incessantly and with longing of steak and fries. Some of them had cell phone contact with family and friends outside. The aquarium suffered significant loss of animal life when the facility's emergency generator failed and made conditions unlivable for most of its animals. The building got a few bumps and bruises, but it held up. The tradition is something which we truly need to imagine that we can remain connected with or even immersed in. And when the worst of the storm had passed, there were corpses all over the city, the stores were being looted, nurses took over on mechanical ventilators and spent many hours on end manually forcing air into the lungs of unconscious patients to keep them alive, there was smoke in the dome, you didn't know if you were going to burn up or if the building was going to fall down around you, there were numerous frightening moments and strange sounds coming from the cement roof; these, in sum, were code words for: if you are poor and black, you are not crossing the river. Two days after the event, the store at the corner remained locked. The dairy display case was clearly visible through the windows, food in it slowly decaying. Through the cracks in the floors rose the stench of the greasy water swirling through the windows below. They designated a storm drain as the bathroom, and the kids built an elaborate enclosure for privacy out of plastic, broken umbrellas and other scraps; the officials responded that they were going to take care of them, and some of them got a sinking feeling. Strangers on the street offered them money and toiletries with words of welcome. They waited for 48 hours for the buses. While wealthy residents fled the city in SUVs, racial politics continued to permeate the social fabric.

A REPRESENTATIVE for a business located in the 2000

block of N___ reports a known 38-40 year old black man who did enter the business via a back door and took a bag of dry cleaned shirts and fled on a bicycle. In the city centre he spent some time trying to find a phone box; when he found an empty one, the receiver was lying on the floor, the wires torn out of their socket. With his eyes closed, he was overcome by a strange inability to visualise anything. A resident of the 200 block of B___ reports a known suspect residing in the 600 block of L___, who did make threatening phone calls to her home to harass, threaten and annoy her in violation of an Order of Protection. And he said that they had made a universal extermination camp the ideal terminus of this whole civilisation. The very structure of the city itself, with the stone container dominating the magnet, may in the past have been in no small degree responsible for this resistance. She reported that he had said to her: "Thou art my glory, and the lifter up of mine head." Flirtation and courtship created those moments of suspense and uncertainty, of blandishment and withdrawal, that serve as safeguards against satiety: a counterpoise to the regimentation of habit. Accordingly, two cities have been formed by two loves, in relatively self-contained and balanced communities, with a sound industrial base. In the one, the princes and the nations it subdues are ruled by the love of ruling; in the other, the princes and the subjects serve one another in love, the latter obeying, while the former take thought for all. Every Human Vegetated Form is in its inward recesses. Though the ruin was widespread, large patches of healthy tissue fortunately remained. Armies, governments, capitalistic enterprises took the characteristic animus and form of this order, in all its inflated dimensions. They became vain in their imaginations, and their foolish heart was darkened; professing themselves to be wise, that is, glorying in their own wisdom, and being possessed by pride. Thus absolute power would become in fact absolute nihilism. Morality would become police. Explosives would reach cosmic violence. Disintegration would overcome integration. But the earthly city, which shall not be everlasting (for it will no longer be a city when it has been committed to the extreme penalty), has its good in this world, and rejoices in it with such joy as such things can afford. You could see a man combing his hair with his fingers, you could see girls moving backwards as they danced, you could see men standing up and buttoning their coats, you could hear the noise the cards made as they were shuffled, but you did not have to dwell on it any more. But as this is not a good which can discharge its devotees of all distresses, this city is often divided against itself by litigations, wars, quarrels, and such victories as are either life-destroying or short-lived. All this had a direct effect upon both old structures and new. For each part of it that arms against another part of it seeks to triumph over the nations though itself in bondage to vice. If, when it has conquered, it is inflated with pride, its victory is life-destroying; but if it turns its thoughts upon the common casualties of our mortal condition, and is rather anxious concerning the disasters that may befall it than elated with the successes already achieved, this victory, though of a higher kind, is still only short-lived; for it cannot abidingly rule over those whom it has victoriously subjugated. A D__ resident reports hearing a loud boom while driving north on G__ Street between B__ and P__ as her rear window exploded into the vehicle. But the things which this city desires cannot justly be said to be evil, for it is itself, in its own kind, better than all other human good. For it desires earthly peace for the sake of enjoying earthly goods, and it makes war in order to attain to this peace; since, if it has conquered, and there remains no one to resist it, it enjoys a peace which it had not while there were opposing parties who contested for the enjoyment of those things which were too small to satisfy both. A resident of the 500 block of N__ reports an unknown person did cut the lock off a garage door to access it and take a lawn-mower worth $28. A resident of O__ L__ Road reports, while at F__ L__ Cemetery, an unknown person did enter the chapel and take his leather strapped satchel containing 3 checkbooks, cash and personal papers, purchased by toilsome wars, obtained by what they style a glorious victory. Now, when victory remains with the party which had the juster cause, who hesitates to congratulate the victor, and style it a desirable peace? These things, then, are good things. But if they neglect the better things of the heavenly city, which are secured by eternal victory and peace never-ending, and so inordinately covet these present good things that they believe them to be the only desirable things, or love them better than those things which are believed to be better – if this be so, then it is necessary that misery follow and ever increase. A D__ resident reports, while at A__ and D__ an unknown black male, 20s, 5'8" and of thin build, who did approach her and say, "How you doing" while running his hand over his head. "When we shall have reached that peace," she said, "this mortal life shall give place to one that is eternal, and our body shall be no more this animal body which by its corruption weighs down the soul, but a spiritual body feeling no want, and in all its members subjected to the will." In its pilgrim state, where the shadow of the helicopter raced across the mottled green surface of the water, the heavenly city possesses this peace by faith; and by this faith it lives righteously when it refers to the attainment of that peace every good action towards God and man; for the life of the city is a social life.

SHE WALKED out of the city, with her cats and luggage in a grocery cart. I'm sure we'll hear from her very soon with more details once she can communicate. She said she was interviewed for Dateline for tonight, so I'll watch and tape if she is. I'm so devastated and happy. This morning I woke up on James' sofa with a cat curled up on my head. I sat up and walked into James' room and we talked. Then, I went and sat outside to watch the antics of three little hummingbirds and a big blue jay. The grass is green. The weather is beautiful. I don't feel so alone. We are drowned, and we know that we shall never die.

5 Bruised Rationals (City of Angels)

YOU GOT it. You got what you paid for (it). You want it, for what, you got the money paid. What for, what they want? What you got, blue screen, she'd break the fiscal, money? It's paid for. Blue you want? Floats on a curve of money that they paid for up on the screen. It's what got the break, the fiscal weather she brought, peaking volumes into a narcotic maul. You want blue? Break in the weather? Fiscal burning? They want that peaking curve she brought to the screen. Up on what do those volumes of money float? Narcotic patterns? Then go into a perfect mall, you paid for it, you got it. They want that peaking curve on the blue screen, or to imagine a lightbulb burning, floating on perfect water, breaking volumes of narcotic patterns. The money you paid is brought to you. Then what? The intention of the weather is ... to destroy intention. For glass descended, unable to go into.... she breaks up. She got fiscal in a mall? You want to go fiscal? To destroy intention, to float? To imagine money peaking, breaking, curving on a glass screen? It's perfect blue water, moving into the realms of the future. It's weather patterns breaking up, or volumes of narcotics in the blood now flowing backwards, descending into heat; not the heat of a lightbulb burning, but sexual in the mall, paid for with what she's got. Unstable or unable? A bird of unknown provenance. Then what? She'd break behind the darkness? Brought to the real, falling out in the perfect city, falling through blue glass, falling through real estate, they know that. Not the heat, not intention, money on glass not moving, not descending, water moving, not breaking, flowing, not to want imagine or destroy, not to imagine perfect blue, no volumes descending, no sexual burning. To go, to float into what the future brought, out and through, not falling in the fiscal dark, they behind, then, or in the weather patterns, that real blue glass, not in the realms of, nor the provenance, not paid for with money or narcotics. An unstable screen breaking up. What blood, what lightbulb? What mall in what perfect city? Unable to what? The estate of the real? But where? Got up where? It's here! It's what you want, in the realms of then, and not brought, not falling to or unable to fall. Not falling, she not falling, not now, not the unknown bird, not peaking, curving backwards, not you.

IT IS whose flows of what may mean not even there was different were in dreams a rush all peaking to incorporate a curve a blue who fail when loved to imagine on screen burning glass through morning something opened and spoke density through the future without regard on water of peaceful conversations like what you got the certain patterns folds you turn you walk you're in the structure meanwhile people don't have dumbly sonorous openings into the conjunction close down the light below the dog but all is love guns have money intention to destroy as happens when a bullet has the heat viewed through and being evidence place spiced blue-screen wisdom brightening he wished that's how blinds turned and he a bird is rich he came they ate the sound there were the women remembered light whole being for all to create don't look

IT IS, after all, what you want, a crisis of the self whose blood now flows backwards. It's a signifier of what? It may not mean, not even…. There were chimes of all sizes and there was information, all tuned to different needs: computers, dolphins and dreams. A cohort of young lesbians were in attendance. They say we dream 40 dreams a night. Narcotics rush into the brain, peaking volumes. Why should they want to incorporate such reluctance? A curve, a perfect blue, don't move. Who can fail to appreciate limbs when they are loved or curved, or to imagine snakes? The fog soon lifted to reveal the cormorants on the rocks below. He had it up on screen but, the reading lamp burning his left hand, she brought a glass of water through an incipient maze of morning glory and crustacea. So of course it was something completely different. He opened the lid and

Those openings into openings "traced for the conjunction of worlds".

spoke into it softly, as though attempting to wake a child. A kind of density through time moves into the realms of the future without regard to perspective, floats on the wrong water like a diagram of a peaceful voyage, and the conversations vanished like that foam. So after all you got what you paid for. You got your break in the uncertain fiscal weather. You are at certain patterns, a whole city white and red, the luminous folds of the fog before a stuffed bulletin board at an unventilated table. You turn into a mall, you walk a few blocks and suddenly you're in Korea. It seems to be clean but the structure has collapsed. A Zen priest floats in a tweed jacket aspiring to laconicity, the others meanwhile approach a "where are they now" situation, and the young people don't have a "thing". Well there's a whole regime of fills, dumbly sonorous, but those openings into openings "traced for the conjunction of worlds" show the darkness never far away. Behind the lightbulb strings – the smell of dust burning on a light-bulb close to Haiti. So he drives down the coast past the real estate, the tables dappled with light and the seabirds on the flat, nothing below the bridge. He loves his dog Suzie dearly but all he's really interested in is death and money; love guns and anti-tank grenades – just so long as they have the right money. The intention of shooting at short range is to destroy the vital centres of the medulla, as happens when a captive bolt is used for slaughtering cattle; a bullet pro-duces a cavity which has a volume several hundred times that of the bullet. Cavitation is probably due to the heat dissipated when the impact of the bullet boils the water and volatile fats in the tissue which it strikes. Lifeguard towers are viewed through blue glasses. He

Lifeguard towers are viewed through blue glasses.

discovered he was gay *and* being sued for sexual harassment. Nowhere is there evidence that these conversations actually took place. When he remembered it, it was like a dream, but when he forgot, it wasn't – it was to do with patterns of blood flow in the brain. What is it? cooked spiced minced beef with just a hint of sewage? Canalised, a filthy trickle behind a blue-screen powerbook – a jerk; worse than a jerk. Wisdom crieth, brightening, solemnly celebrated – she'd break if not, utters. Exactly how the tables turned he didn't know, she did it and he wished she hadn't. That's how it breaks: the curved, painted horses going round and round, a national monument. Blinds turned, screen blank, everybody falling to, falling out today – not in terms of technique but of information. And he was quoting directly, it's insane! A bird in a blanket, a blue bird of unknown provenance. The soil is rich, and supports an abundance of flowering plants and fruit trees: several kinds of peach, apricot, oranges, lemons and others. He came initially to study for a year, and ended up staying permanently, in a city where permanence is unknown, whose capacity to render void or at least unstable any sense of identity or of comfort is well documented, where the FedEx man passes up and down the street bearing jiffy bags. They wandered around, ate hamburger, bought socks and CDs, then headed up to the hills to see the world all spread out beneath, framed softly by light smog. Indy rock on the sound system, a shabby assorted collection, mustard, leather, terrible coffee, duct, fan. And lo, the library descended onto the hilltop and there perched, a thing of glass and steel. And there were zebra striped walls and violet strip lightning strobing at 50 Hz, mirrors and black beer, limes, chili dip and grey meat. The women were too beautiful and they didn't go to work. He had a feeling he remembered great white spaces, big light. It's part of your whole being. For all of our sakes. Unable to create file. Go quickly, don't look back....

6 City on the Marshes

WATER. SAND. Clay. Time. Vernacular brick. They remembered. Some remains. Overhead creaks. At night. Dark rain. Beech gleamed. It was. A circling helicopter. The Tigris supermarket. The waiting area. It was time. The hysterical girls. They remembered this. Did it exist? Had it existed? Water streaming down. It was sand. Bumps and scrapes. They recalled sand. The deserted ballroom. A discarded mattress. The building disappeared. The thresholds cracked. Tapping on metal. Many dismal events. It was gold. Aqueous grey sky. Even the birds. A doner kebab. Conditions were extremely localised. Chimes in the wind. The whole building rumbled. Did they dream it? Diabolical liberties were took. They cracked the sink. Hints of anti-capitalist activity. It was all sand. Humps for 700 yards. Big trucks clanking slowly. Industrial sounds all night.

Humps for 300 yards. Ghosts on the common. They had imagined it. Acres of high teak. It was only matter. A sheen on windscreens. Dreaming of the Peloponnese. Everything they touched became transparent. A rising star, light pollution. Boom of the bass upstairs. Obdurate clay at the bottom. Water running down the walls. A small, dark animal, quivering. Water pouring down the walls. How they all got soaked. They had imagined the city. Signal failures in all directions. A strong smell of burning. They saw the police cordons. Smoke hung in the air. They recalled loud, quick African voices. Waking to central heating and Elgar. A man screaming in the street. Morning fog that never entirely cleared. Passengers waiting in line without ambition. An ancient dog lay near them. Unseemly scrambles for vacant bus seats. Buildings being constructed for unknown purposes. A vast pool of undrained water. There was a defective train ahead. The basement was packed, stuffy, glaring. Flawlessly polished readings in the gallery. The stadium resplendent as twilight gathered. The springy turf at the conclusion. Bird, traffic and aircraft sounds, intermittent. They especially liked the exploded church. The Kingdom Hall of Jehovah's Witnesses. Of course, there was no signposting.

IT WAS only a matter of time. A vista of dismal interiors, harshly lit. Here was a picture of Russian dolls. A fine smog made their eyes water. One city, one zone from 4 January. The wreck of the next door garden. The supply of used mattresses seemed inexhaustible. Wind chimes banging against the bedroom window.

He was spied lurking with a bird. Poor air quality, liquid condensed on skin. Indifferent pub lunch by the crowded river. Someone talked at length about cash flow. It was rather lost in the acoustics. Text in saline, in a dense mash. Part of the park had been flooded. Ducks, dogs and footballers were the principal inhabitants. The city spoke in noise clusters, lingered thunderously. Vernacular yellow brick stained by generations of salts. Yellow was the colour of the CCTV cameras. A car-park of a different colour, blistering fast. A woman changed her socks on the train. The new library with its proud iconic sign. Monteverdi, Radiohead and John Coltrane at the workstation. The place had been thoroughly cleaned and degreased. Newly appointed as librarian, he suddenly acquired gravitic mass. A dense forest of scaffolding obscured the turning. Speckled with snow, and dust from the works. A slick of biriani clinging to the pavement. The damp smell created by sparse fat raindrops. They saw the comet in the north-west sky. Already the heating was on for short periods. They "flew through the day with sugar-free wings". They were pitching chilling microtones and sweet harmonies. The war was not going nearly so well. Sunshine in the basin, and shadow in the crypt. Some of those glassy buildings had never been occupied. Chainlink fencing had been erected around the never-ending works. Blocks of air to breathe in between the bricks. They could find nowhere to buy a humble lightbulb. They reassembled the Dexion shelving in the mysterious corridor. Silently, the giant wheel stood in the evening light. They remembered it as laden with objects and status. Thunder, and sheeting rain, then a lighted bus passed.

A monk, or possibly a madman, boarded the bus. One of the water tanks fell through the roof. The park had turned fresh once more following rain. The dog walkers and bird feeders were out again. Three serious joggers followed each other at long intervals. The viola player said: "You've had you ears lowered." After a while, they no longer took any notice. Rubbish began to pile by the pub wall again. Many yellow, brown and gold leaves on the ground. A pie and mash lunch before Monteverdi's *Return of Ulysses*. They settled in the front row before the ludicrous proscenium. They were incredibly casual, operating in a sort of half-kitchen. This heat drives people to kill, asserted the picture editor. He hung in his plexiglas box, persecuted by drunken sceptics. About 40 people clustered into three-quarters of a small bare-boarded room. The woman's performing voice sounded like a tape being played backwards. They started off with "analogue sources", but could have ended earlier. Their hands empty of maps, they had returned from the shops. Delays were attributed to a defective train earlier at this station. Waiting around most of the week in the L-shaped assembly area. They heard that it was "not a question of *if* but *when*". How leaning against the doors again prevented the "train from motoring". A man in a white coat climbed into a wheelie bin. The area was now of course crawling with fluorescent jacketed police. Water was pouring through the bathroom ceiling via the light fittings. They experienced disappointment as another mattress was deposited on the greensward. The moon stood in the day's afterglow above the furniture warehouse. They remembered, but the memory itself then became a forgotten thing.

Delays were attributed to a defective train earlier at this station.

Three taps on the window, but nobody on the fire escape. The tidal rhythms of refrigerators in every flat in the block. A sudden gust of wind outside, flinging hailstones against the glass. One of them shattered and was displayed afterwards in bloody pieces. Having to use upward of two night buses to get home. How amber light from the blazing car made the shadows wobble violently. The huge branches of the roadside plane tree swinging in the wind. Being trapped in dock-lands among property, lacking a workstation or any direction. Stomach queasy and hot, morale very low as the regions were abolished. Conversations of besuited persons of both sexes at lunchtime, empty and amusing. One said "That's a matter of conjecture" quite loudly in the garden. Another said: "If they're helping Africans, they might as well help me." They pretended to be on a package holiday in their own neighbourhood. It was a "bring a work of art, take one away" do. Radio people with their tall mikes were waiting to do the interviews. They particularly delighted in the body language of the artist known as "Wobble". It was very Scandinavian, blond and chrome, but the lifts were being deconstructed. Artworks projected onto a suspended sheet, striated by light from the venetian blind. One performer showed everybody his penis, flickering briefly against a "no-signal" video screen. The food was good, if expensive, the outlook over the glittering river magical. The wine was kept in a plastic rubbish bin, packed with ice cubes. But all too soon, it was cold outside, and birdsong could be heard. Dark shadows, yellow light seeping, but a pale sky prepared to precipitate rain. Fear of widespread rail disruption following an incident at a major railway terminus. Fear of plung-

The tidal rhythms of refrigerators in every flat in the block.

ing into the rush hour once again, mowing down homecoming schoolchildren. There was an industrial tang to the air, a diesel aroma that lingered. Most of the damage was done in a swift spell when the shape collapsed. Below the surface was a narrow, damp-smelling tube faced with white ceramic tiles. Water streamed down the walls; years later, the yellow streaks remained as testimony. Surfaces were built up, then partially removed, destroyed, burnt through, leaving evidence, tracings, traces. A tour behind the scenes revealed distinctly industrial looking ducts, stores and floodgates underground. Up above there were continuous rumbling noises as of bodies being endlessly wheeled around. A sheen on windscreens, a shabby teddy bear affixed to the top of scaffolding. Corrections, negotiations, a trip to the copy shop as the temperature dipped once more. In the bank, the two-year-old's mother snarled: "Close your legs, you're a girl child!" It was only a matter of time before things would come to a head. That day, everybody tried to log onto news websites, which slowed to a standstill. The orange-back-lit dummy fireman in the first-storey window endlessly gestured to the passing traffic. A flock of seagulls was illuminated briefly by the yellow uplights outside the concert-hall. Many dismal events above pubs were recalled in which no books had been sold. A man in the training room said: "I seen a clink in the market." He couldn't feel his feet and his shoulders were aching from carrying his briefcase.

TEARING UP the old carpet had revealed a nest of paperclips, cotton buds and buttons. A young man had

Fear of widespread rail disruption following an incident at a major railway terminus.

been apprehended on the landing attempting to remove the security door. The entrance to the bin area was flooded, so they sent for the drain doctor. Music formed part of the ambience and integrated with the structure of the vast building. They had imagined the city before ever seeing it, before being driven from the docks. The endless repetition: "Bus stopping at next bus stop – please stand well clear of doors." Everyone was absorbed: in paperback novels, a tiny, leather-bound Bible, tabloid newspapers, earphone sound-worlds, thoughts. They lost the chance, they did not gain 500 any time any network voice minutes. The quavering tone and the lack of definite articles or active verbs quickly became unendurable. Graffiti, meaning-less to everyone save the original engraver, were painstakingly etched into the window glass. It took three hours to get home, drenched and cold, by train and two buses. Did they dream that they had been in a city that was an open toilet? A black man on the bus said "You need a licence to touch someone's face." "Severe fucking bonehead" – the verdict of a football supporter on the train with obvious racist sympathies. Outside the furniture warehouse, a man was heard to say "I'm going to fucking shoot you." He was a man in his forties who played guitar and sang about unattain-able young women. The colour of his skin was greyish yellow, but it was surprisingly warm to the touch. The air was an unspecific threat, a kind of disembodied life form that roamed the city. Some of the young trees lining the diagonal path still had a heavy freight of blossom. Momentary, irrational anxiety as a helicopter ambulance drifted backwards in the air, roaring just yards overhead. Loud male African voices boomed from the park, whose lawn had been shaved and was yellowing fast. The festival on the park was a sort of counter-celebration, except that this was not made explicit. Eagerly, the small white dog leapt to the fullest extent of his leash, his owner quite indifferent. The small fat child danced on the pavement before his mum; later, he roared, like a pig. At close to 3 in the morning, the isolated sound of birdsong in the lane was heard. A feeding frenzy of bluetits and great tits in the early morning light outside the bedroom window. A great glass and steel building appeared almost overnight on what had previously been waste ground.

BRUNCH IN the executive lounge (steak, bacon, sausage, scrambled eggs, coffee and Bucks Fizz) before the event. Acres of polished parquet flooring, high teak panelling and a huge bay window, incandescent behind the stage. Each place had a white pad and a white pencil with the logo of the advertising agency. In the men's toilet was a machine that dispensed condoms of all flavours, including curry and lager-and-lime. T-shirted thugs placed the stacking chairs in rows as fast as people were able to thread through. A bunch were milling round waiting for the mysterious cellar room to be vacated by the Masons. In search of pianos, they went walking in the heights, marvelling, and dubbing the neighbourhood "Golden Handcuff Land". They remembered a sand-coloured evening sky pierced by the silver of building-site arc-lights and gold of street lamps. A selection of 1- and 2-bed apartments and 2- and 3-bed town houses was shortly to be released. An office the size of a football pitch, conical-topped buildings visible through polarised glass, metal of unknown provenance. How the sounds of the traffic had hard edges around them, almost as though they were being hallucinated. A supermarket trolley loaded with cabbages was being deftly wheeled out of the way of an approaching bus. People wheel wheeled objects in the street at one in the morning for goodness' sake, she remarked bitterly. On the other bus, a woman and a schoolgirl came to blows in a dispute over personal space. The bus had to terminate here because the bus driver was a novice and had lost his way. In an entertaining performance he had parodied Nietzsche and Eastern mysticism while making good use of a flipchart. Because a mother had spilt paint on the exit platform, the bus had been taken out of service. A girl on the bus: "Proper vexed – the only time I weren't vexed was when I saw you." Drenched people, multiracial and apparently mostly poor, were allowed in at last to an auction of liquidated stock. Something could have been rescued out of that sludge, but only if some objectivity about it was achieved. It was a street-market performance precisely engineered to get people to part with money for things they didn't want. A girl with a good smell but an off-hand manner sold her spare ticket to someone in the queue. But when they got to the shopping centre they decided it was one of the inner circles of hell. They asked for a cup of tea, which the owner wouldn't sell them unless they were also buying food. A dozen high cranes were employed in building the new stadium, pinpoint lights on them piercing the afternoon gloom. They cowered in the study as the deconstructors drilled and hammered terrifyingly just outside the blacked-out bathroom and kitchen windows. Hammer blows caused tiles to fall off the bathroom wall. The only viable idea was to raise the monster water tank by a couple of feet within the airing cupboard. All the trappings were slowly stripped away, until the bare boards and the light on the horizon were arrived at. Soon the snow had disappeared, and it was a sunny morning, gold light on the treetrunks, dreamy sounds of traffic. The covers had been whipped away from the kitchen window by the wind, so light came in there at last. On the balcony, major rubbish had accumulated: a sad kitchen cabinet, crumbling, an old standard lamp, a burnt-out vacuum cleaner. A pile of bathroom fittings and other debris left on the shrubbery. There appeared to be little or no furniture, though charred toothbrushes were seen through the window on the bathroom ledge. Towards dusk, the raucous calls of three crows flying frantically around and through and between the trees of the park. There was a huge yellow moon on the eastern horizon, while Mars was still clearly visible in the southern sky. Now the rain returned, in darkness outside, and a cat's brief cry, the garden partly roped off with warning tape.

NEXT DAY, another office, further south and higher, a lone hubcap framed on the wall, curry stains on the mouse mat. For weeks, the same wad of used chewing gum, showing no sign of deterioration, had remained within the men's first-floor urinal. A small dark turd was once found on the floor next to the toilet bowl in the same facility at HQ. They remembered the Muslim men with trays of brightly coloured phone cards for

Towards dusk, the raucous calls of three crows flying frantically around and through and between the trees of the park.

sale on upturned crates outside the station entrance. They remembered the performance by two female colleagues, making language do impossible things and rushing in and out of several rooms. Their sleep was disrupted in the early hours of the morning by comings and goings in the flat across the landing. The clouds were completely absent first thing in the morning, and then later came upon it stealthily and bunched and became grey. A litter of pekinese pups were taken out for exercise as usual, some on leads, the smaller ones packed into a pram. They remembered times spent partly sitting on a bench in the midst of the park's oceanic tracts of grass, circled by dogs. Two boys said there was a fire behind the men's toilets and a man with white hair confirmed that a bush was burning. A white man with a blotchy face and close-cropped hair moved in upstairs and he and his mates were heard daily, banging and drilling. He had been moved into a better room, with a view over the car park rather than of the wall of the boiler room. The day the Hoover burnt out he was seen in the pub with a couple of well-dressed strangers. They remembered waking up to golden sunshine filtering through slats and lighting up the Japanese lantern, and thinking they were in a palace, or paradise. Her new piano nestling in the bay overlooking the garden, glowing in the early morning light while sounds of kids playing and screaming drifted in. Lying face upward in the osteopath's consulting room, looking at a small square of sky above the roller blind, and deciding to cling to that. Time spent among grey, ultramarine and orange glass buildings, all of them empty, mirroring an empty world, the attractive light railway winding sharply between them. Deadheaded daffodils; sculpted bollards, rust-patined; magnolia blossom from the tree at the corner of King's on the Rye carpeting a whole corner of the grass. From the bus on a fine spring morning, watching the rush-hour crowds scurrying to work, the only sound being Ligeti's *Lux Aeterna* on the headphones. Friday evenings outside the pub: the wooden benches filling up, the sky pale, grass pale, conversation feverish, as though an event was about to happen. Clacking of shears wielded by an elderly man clipping a hedge – scent of the clippings, a ponderous screech of bus brakes at a pedestrian crossing. How the cat was buried in thin soil above obdurate clay at the bottom of the garden, and how a fox subsequently dug her up. On the floor behind was detritus, and amid this a quantity of unmistakeable droppings and an animal urine smell that had come to seem familiar. Someone had stolen the front bicycle wheel and substituted one with a bigger radius that didn't fit, and anyway had a flat tyre. The air was an unspecific threat, a kind of disembodied life form that roamed the city silently, hunting for victims, rendering them invisible, or nowhere. The city made its own music, which travelled from deep within it; there were sounds in that ocean that no human had ever heard. A foreign, wailing woman descended, not understanding the voice that said northbound trains were suspended, and then demanding to be taken to the alternative bus service. People averted their faces when a man, running for a bus, tripped on a loop of wire and fell sprawling with his briefcase in the gutter. The woman lost her temper and started cursing in a German accent: "What the fuck do you know about Frank Zappa?" was the gist of

The air was an unspecific threat, a kind of disembodied life form
that roamed the city.

it. In the café across the road, a picture of the Niagara falls, in which the glowing waters appeared to move, provided the electricity was switched on. A crow chose its moment to divebomb a cat as it was making a break across the road – almost causing it to collide with a cyclist. Mid-winter flashed by, the sun popped out and now foxes fucked on a piece of waste ground behind the railway embankment – they heard the vixen's screams. Grey fog laid over scrub on a whitish park; suddenly a herd of deer appeared without noise, their big eyes staring, while steam rose between the saplings. A large fox, greyish in the sodium lamplight, bounded swiftly across the road in front of the hotel and disappeared into the darkness of the park opposite. The Glengall Tavern, The Globe, The Greyhound, The Red Bull, The Clayton Arms, The Hope, The Heaton Arms, The White Horse, The Rye Hotel, The Clock House. In the Paper Mill, straining to hear and screaming to be heard above the music, a few of them left and those getting fewer clustered more closely. Who was the only other person in the cinema to get the joke when the Brad Pitt character pronounced the Marquis de Sade "Shah-deh", like the singer? In the lane, which was filled with bright sunshine, a crowd of Muslim men and boys in white shirts, some embracing each other, held up the traffic. The oriental shops they remembered from their previous visit seemed to have long gone, as part of the inexorable drift of tourist traps towards global corporate homogeneity. A man showed them an envelope containing what purported to be the remains of a scorpion; it turned out to be a practical joke that didn't work. It was pleasant enough in the garden at the centre of the square, normally

The Rye Hotel.

closed to the general public, saying farewell over fras-
cati, chicken legs and baby quiches. Too warm and
stuffy to take sound into another direction in the upper
room of the pub; but a self-destructing poem at least
did not outstay its welcome. After brief discussion outside the pub, they concluded that dread is when you
have to go to work, and angst is when you don't, but
have no money. At the top of the escalator each
evening, the homeless boy held up a magazine in one
hand, offering it for sale as though it were the sacra-
ment. They were exhorted to stand well clear of the
closing doors; advised not to place their persons or
belongings or the smooth functioning of the system in
jeopardy. A great mound of rubbish lay outside the
front door: old clothes, a filthy carpet underlay laden
with orange brick-dust, grubby woollen rug, a motor-
bike helmet, an umbrella. Later, unseen in the warm
dark garden, the three-legged cat betrayed its presence
with a faint tinkle from its collar, a familiar and com-
forting sound in the stillness. The sound of a piano
late at night from a neighbouring window, played by an
elderly man from the Balkans known by everyone
locally to be profoundly deaf. It was not until he
turned round to put on his coat at the end of the
evening that he became aware there was nobody at the
keyboard. Meanwhile, a bus blew up a few hundred
yards away, killing one man, said on the news later to
have probably been the bomber, and badly injuring
four others. They passed a yard wherein three vans, in
states of disrepair, were almost submerged in detritus
of all kinds: bricks, planks, pieces of scaffolding, rusting tools, traffic cones, rubble. Another yard packed
with hibernating ice-cream vans. In the centre of the

city, dozens of police vehicles were parked at the kerb-side and hundreds of policemen in fluorescent yellow jackets patrolled meaningfully in the intermittent rain. In the supermarket, an old woman who had what looked like a growth on her face, the skin around it being yellowy-green, giving the impression her face was collapsing. On the bus, a man with a baby's dummy in his mouth, held on a cord round his neck, said "508" with a look of bruised grandeur on his face. A young woman squatting between parked cars, jeans pulled down, peeing, being remonstrated with by an elderly homeless man, shouted back: "I don't see why they think it's so funny." Every morning the old woman with the sick dog took it out of its travelling basket in the park, where, followed by marauding crows, it would do its business briefly. A crane swung an iron ball repeatedly at a remaining brick wall, while a bulldozer busied itself on the mountain of rubble and a bonfire of planking blazed through the mist. The builders had gone bankrupt, it appeared, leaving the fire escapes half done, and the security man posted outside each day was there to stop them coming back to steal materials. Animal cries and bird calls, distant train whistle and the rush of an incoming wave, brief interludes of utter mayhem, long moments of con-trolled beauty – at least, that was the idea. Someone had transported a traditional river barge to moor at the quayside between the office buildings, but after some time it had sunk because nobody realised it had to be maintained. They were disappointed to discover the warehouse district near one of the many river bridges, once redolent of spices, had been transformed into a complex of boutiques, wine bars and high-priced apartments. A man with stumps for teeth, wearing a girlie T-shirt nuzzled a small black cat as he boarded the bus, speaking to it in reassuring tones and kissing it when it whimpered. They recalled the crowds were threaded, three by three, up the wooden spiral staircase with its vertical rope banister, through the surgical museum under the rafters and into the tiny operating theatre. One of the women shot water at a boiling kettle to cool its strident blast, while an "empty" film was projected onto the wall beyond, interfered with by the shadow of steam. They wore uniformly dark suits; one of them endlessly chalked scribbles on a blackboard while the smell of burning wax from two paschal candles began to permeate the space, altering its shape. (When the roof started to catch fire, that was not part of the performance.) What it felt like was baroque music or jazz at the time of its creation; that is, when the protagonists collectively had little idea of what it was called or what the boundaries were. Elsewhere, a man who looked as though he'd been put together from spare parts was amiable, as was his poetry – but he was of the school that prefaces each poem with an amusing anecdote. Ripples spread majestically across the breadth of the branches of the great plane tree across the road, swaying symphonically as the wind caught it, then moments later becoming still again before the next gust. A thunderstorm was predicted, and duly arrived just after midnight, crashing dramatically almost overhead for not more than a few minutes, flashing golden-white light through the curtains and bringing with it sudden torrential rain.

THAT MORNING an overweight man in a T-shirt and dark slacks came out of the baker's swinging a French stick sheathed in custom-made clear plastic; he tripped on a paving stone and the sheathed bread skipped. A familiar old woman in a fawn raincoat, headscarf and old wellington boots shuffled very slowly up the road past the park, pushing a shopping trolley, and stopping every couple of minutes for a long rest. There was scarcely anybody about, the houses seemed uninhabited, even the birds had been silenced, the weather was greyly oppressive; for all they knew, everyone had been carried off by a plague or a silent invasion. She was asked whether she would prefer the Cardinal, only walking distance away but with dull food and ambience, or the New Inn, a car ride but nicer; to which she replied instantly, "I'd prefer to die." An elderly black man on the underground train picked up a copy of a newspaper that had been left on the seat, muttered half to himself, "Twenty t'ousand dead – what purpose?" more than once before tossing it aside. A man carrying a black rucksack gestured across the street at an unseen person, possibly the driver of the bus they were on, tapping his finger on his forehead to indicate insanity, and then spitting, or simulating spitting. Then he made his excuses and slipped across the river to listen to a man roaring around the room, pausing to sonically trace the contours of a Patrick Caulfield print – the attendant pretending not to be concerned. A curious setting, like a school stage, a high platform, wood panelling behind to a height of seven feet, and above that blood orange walls, and the performers coming out of doors in the scenery at the back. On the way back, he was interrupted by a young woman calling out to him, asking the time; upon being told, she immediately asked, in the same singsong, yet deadpan voice: "Can I come and live with you?" All evening, a strong smell of burning slowly became more and more pervasive; then in the morning an aluminium pan appeared on the ground next to the bins, which on closer inspection contained a mass of charred ex-food. They relived a walk through the cemetery, along the canal to a pub with a view of the great sweep of the river, buildings glinting, seagulls skimming, and then on to the customary Indian restaurant and several Kingfisher beers. It was spotting with rain and the air suddenly became laden and dense over the trees, then there was a tremendous flash of lightning maybe yards away, followed almost immediately by a huge thunderclap – after that, the air cleared. (They were told there were no trains because lightning had struck the signal box.) Another day, having locked himself out of the flat when embarking on a walk over the common to the takeaway, he had to ask the man for a plastic spoon with which to eat his biriani on a park bench. The flat had been devastated by fire – a sack of garden rubbish by the gate had been charred, and on top of it was the burnt-out frame of an armchair, which appeared to have been flung out of the window. A constant, unnamed fear was experienced – or rather, an intermittent one, disappearing from consciousness for long periods and only being triggered by apprehension of an unusual moment, such as a customer in the throng stooping to inspect his own shoe. While he was waiting under the railway bridge for the bus, a van roared up and a man leaned out, appearing to aim a missile at him, which turned out to be a black floppy disk that clattered on the pavement. "Is he a communist?" the question was posed, to which the answer, "No he ain't, he's just using religion to cover his disgusting acts", came amid the aroma of vinegar, or more properly, non-grape condiment, deliquescing on a portion of chips. Sunday morning: the Jehovah's witnesses arrived for their service in their Fords and BMWs, middle class black couples, occasionally white folk, occasionally single people, few children; they parked their cars on the yellow lines and the men took out their briefcases. They remembered the deep-voiced, square woman in a dress and wool hat who chanted about Jesus at the bus stop outside the train station daily; and how fewer people each day remarked on her presence, until at last acceptance or indifference prevailed. At one point the train was being backed up a few yards in order to then build up enough speed to get it over the next gradient; but eventually, this ploy failed, and it died about 200 yards short of the station. More than 40 people crammed into the back space of the bookshop for the launch, including those who'd wandered in off the street and stayed, and a dog that howled softly when one of the poets spoke the line "the dog's death". An Irish drunk addressed a pile of rubbish in the passage between the train station and the office building with an improvised ballad: "Oh the streets of the city / Such a dreadful sight / They're filled with papers / And other shite...." Bedding, Rugs, Kitchen Utensils, Toiletries, Mobile Phone Accessories, Kashmir Halal Butchers, Elnamic House of Fashion (To God Be The Glory), Big Girl Specialists in Large Sizes, African & European Cosmetics, Hair Products, Jewellers, African Videos & Audio (CD's, DVD's), Spiritual Products,

Aromatherapy Products. Approaching the bridge, the bus was delayed in a traffic jam for some time, the reason becoming apparent when it finally crossed the bridge: an army of police had set up a roadblock, including about a dozen policemen and women armed with submachine guns. Close by the station the homeless magazine vendor, after grumbling he was doing so badly in the cold he'd "rather go back to thieving", refused a sale, muttering "I ain't got no change" as he returned the proffered coin and grabbed back the magazine. A dog on a lead, and fat marker pens lined up in his breast pocket. They considered how they never saw the young people upstairs in daylight, nor heard more than faint rumblings within; but they would come to life as midnight approached, and then there were comings and goings and door bangings until maybe five in the morning. Following the collision, the couple abandoned their car, the man aiming a couple of blows first, with a motorcycle helmet he was carrying, at the driver of the van involved in the incident, then they both ran away down the street and never came back. Alone in the gloomy, deserted ballroom, the only one to turn up at the session had started improvising on his instrument (never having done this before), and continued for about 45 minutes, afterwards reporting it to be the most liberating experience of his life. Crossing the rye at dusk, on the way back from a visit to the library, the glimmer of frosty turf all around, he passed two black men in heavy coats midway on the path, while in the left-hand distance the lights of the traffic moved without cease. In the park, a black pit bull terrier hung by its teeth from a dangling tree branch, swinging back and forth for some time before falling to the ground, then leaping up to repeat the performance; its owner, a grey-bearded man in a fawn blouson, watched proudly. He observed a crow fall upon an injured pigeon, and start tearing chunks out of it while it still flapped its wings, the movements becoming less vigorous and finally ceasing; an hour later, some remains and a cloud of feathers were visible, but the following day there was no sign. On the bus, a small boy exclaimed, "Hey, there's Leroy's girlfriend!" whereupon he and his friend wound down a window and shouted below in unison "Leroy's girlfriend!" – but on getting no response the first turned round to his friend and observed, "She ain't Leroy's girlfriend, she's too small for Leroy!" Next evening, while waiting for a No 12 bus home, a man came straight towards them walking exactly along the line of the kerb; when he got close he stopped dead, staring at them, and when, feeling uncomfortable, they moved away, he screamed "shit" at them, then continued along the kerb. He seemed to be a businessman in a suit and tie, with shaven head and chin; then he started acting strangely, counting a great wad of banknotes, and it had become apparent that, despite his smart suit, he was wearing no socks, furthermore, that his hands were incredibly filthy, smeared with what looked like printing ink. Earlier, he had banged on the door, making a big fuss of a puddle of water on his bathroom floor, and insisting on going upstairs to harangue a pair of bemused Indian builders about the tenant, a mysterious "Mr Pensard" , while his pale blonde girlfriend, allegedly a surgeon who had once saved his life, nodded mutely. He was last seen on the platform looking anxiously at the destination indicator. Hard to recall the perceptions that burgeoned into consciousness at certain instants of the day then faded back into non-being: broken bricks at the side of the path leading up to the publishing office; the combination on the entryphone keypad, memorised as a visual pattern; the faint aroma from the toilets at the foot of the stairs. Four tanks were ranged at the back of the stage, at first covered by drapes, but then each in turn was brought forward at various points in the drama, to reveal that they contained, respectively: a model city (which burned down); a bunch of giant toadstools; a collection of flasks of specimens; and finally, pure glittering water. Bright sunshine suddenly turned to foreboding gloom; then there was a ferocious hailstorm for about five minutes, rattling loudly and alarmingly against the windowpanes before abruptly stopping, converting the street and back yard into instant snowscapes; and when sunshine eventually returned there were still thick piles of hailstones the size of gobstoppers to be seen, accumulated in shadowed areas.

THEY RECALLED how a new perfume seemed suddenly to become fashionable, such that every so often they caught a whiff of it in a crowded street, on a bus, in the queue for the station lift, a repugnantly fruity, overripe sort of smell, like that of rotting peaches; and how, much later, just as suddenly, it ceased to be popular and vanished completely. When the doors of the ancient lift failed to open at the bottom, the customers waited silently for almost five minutes, pretending this wasn't happening, before someone shyly suggested pushing the alarm

Someone else would move into that flat eventually, and the
story would start from zero again.

button; upon which the alarm rang harshly and incessantly and could not be turned off throughout the entire time the lift was being winched up, almost imperceptibly slowly, to the top again. Outside the shop where they had gone to buy a new vacuum cleaner, a man had fallen to the pavement, for unknown reasons, and struck his head on the kerb; he was quite still and greyish, a dark stain and a small smear of vomit on the ground round his head, and a woman was giving him mouth-to-mouth resuscitation while a crowd stood around. The bus ground to a halt because a man in a car ahead coming in the opposite direction refused to back up and let it past, even though there was plenty of room for him to do so; becoming aggressive, he got out of his car and shouted and gesticulated at the bus driver, then got back in and started shouting into a mobile phone. At night, they watched from a window overlooking the street: the terrace on the right, the park on the left, a skip stationed at the kerb, then a vast pool of undrained water, two parked cars and a white van, a black and white cat trotting across the road, making for the Paladin shelter, all-night TV reflected in window-glass, the images leaping ceaselessly above everything. The commotion upstairs turned out to be the young solicitor and another man breaking into the neighbour's flat; it was said that he had died a couple of weeks ago, in hospital of a stroke while his now pregnant girlfriend was "up north", thus rendering meaningless all that fuss about the water leak and the building works; and as for the intrigues and threats and byzantine stories nobody had been able to get to the bottom of, all that had vanished into the air; someone else would move into that flat eventually, and the story would start from zero again. It was only a matter of time.

IN THE morning, sunshine, with faint streaks of high cloud; sun flashing off parked car windows opposite putting spots in everyone's vision; in the area of the park where traditionally people would walk their dogs, a man with dark skin, long dark hair, white shirt, black trousers, ambled slowly with hands clasped behind his back, like the monarch's consort on an official visit, his head bowed as though in solemn contemplation, though with no sign of a canine companion; and a blonde woman in jeans and a child in black top and white skirt appeared with a German shepherd, which squatted briefly to shit in the grass, then scampered.

In the morning, sunshine, with faint streaks of high cloud.

Poetry series

1993

Kelvin Corcoran: *Lyric Lyric,* £5.99

Susan Gevirtz: *Taken Place,* £6.50

Maggie O'Sullivan: *In the House of the Shaman*, £6.50

Denise Riley: *Mop Mop Georgette*, £6.50

1994

Allen Fisher: *Dispossession and Cure,* £6.50

1995

Fanny Howe: *O'Clock,* £6.50

Sarah Kirsch: *T* (O/P)

Peter Riley: *Distant Points* (O/P)

1996

Maggie O'Sullivan (ed.): *Out of Everywhere,* £12.50

1997

Nicole Brossard: *Typhon Dru,* £5.50

Cris Cheek/Sianed Jones: *Songs From Navigation* (+ audio CD), £12.50

Lisa Robertson: *Debbie: an Epic,* £7.50*

Maurice Scully: *Steps,* £6.50

1998

Barbara Guest: *If So, Tell Me* (O/P)

2000

Tony Lopez: *Data Shadow,* £6.50

Denise Riley: *Selected Poems,* £7.50

2001

Anselm Hollo (ed. & tr.): *Five From Finland,* £7.50

Lisa Robertson: *The Weather,* £7.50*

2003

Ken Edwards: *eight + six,* £7.50

Robert Sheppard: *The Lores,* £7.50

Lawrence Upton: *Wire Sculptures,* £5

2004

David Miller: *Spiritual Letters (I-II),* £6.50

Redell Olsen: *Secure Portable Space,* £7.50

Peter Riley: *Excavations,* £9

2005

Allen Fisher: *Place,* £15

Tony Baker: *In Transit,* £7.50

2006
   Jeff Hilson: *stretchers*, £7.50
   Maurice Scully: *Sonata*, £8.50
   Maggie O'Sullivan, *Body of Work,* £15
2007
   Sarah Riggs: *chain of minuscule decisions in the form of a feeling*, £7.50
   Carol Watts, *Wrack*, £7.50
   Jeff Hilson (ed.): *The Contemporary Free Verse Sonnet*, £15

* co-published with New Star Books, Vancouver, BC

4Packs series

1996
   1: *Sleight of Foot* (Miles Champion, Helen Kidd, Harriet Tarlo, Scott Thurston), £5
1998
   2: *Vital Movement* (Andy Brown, Jennifer Chalmers, Mike Higgins, Ira Lightman), £5
1999
   3: *New Tonal Language* (Patricia Farrell, Shelby Matthews, Simon Perril, Keston Sutherland), £5
2002
   4: *Renga+* (Guy Barker, Elizabeth James/Peter Manson, Christine Kennedy), £5

Narrative series

1998
   Ken Edwards: *Futures* (O/P)
2005
   John Hall: *Apricot Pages,* £6.50
   David Miller: *The Dorothy and Benno Stories,* £7.50
   Douglas Oliver: *Whisper 'Louise',* £15

Go to www.realitystreet.co.uk, email info@realitystreet.co.uk or write to the address on the reverse of the title page for updates.

BECOME A REALITY STREET SUPPORTER!

Since 1998, nearly 100 individuals and organisations have helped Reality Street Editions by being Reality Street Supporters. Those signed up to the Supporter scheme in 2007 are listed below . The Supporter scheme is an important way to keep Reality Street's programme of adventurous writing alive. When you sign up as a Supporter for a year, you receive all titles published in that year, and your name is printed in the back of the books, as below (unless you prefer anonymity). For more information, go to www.realitystreet.co.uk or email info@realitystreet.co.uk

Peter Barry
Andrew Brewerton
Clive Bush
John Cayley
Adrian Clarke
Kelvin Corcoran
Ian Davidson
Mark Dickinson
Michael Finnissy
Allen Fisher/Spanner
Sarah Gall
Harry Gilonis &
Elizabeth James
Chris Goode
Paul Griffiths
Charles Hadfield
John Hall
Alan Halsey
Robert Hampson
Dylan Harris
Fanny Howe
Piers Hugill
Romana Huk
Peter Jaeger
Lisa Kiew
Peter Larkin
Tony Lopez
Chris Lord
Aodhan McCardle
Ian McMillan
Richard Makin
Michael Mann

Deborah Meadows
Mark Mendoza
Peter Middleton
Geraldine Monk
Stephen Mooney
Maggie O'Sullivan
Marjorie Perloff
Pete & Lyn
Peter Philpott
Tom Quale
Peter Quartermain
Lou Rowan
Will Rowe
Anthony Rudolf
Barry Schwabsky
Maurice Scully
Robert Sheppard
John Shreffler
Peterjon & Yasmin Skelt
Hazel Smith
Valerie & Geoffrey Soar
Harriet Tarlo
Barry Tebb/Sixties Press
Tony Trehy
Catherine Wagner
Sam Ward
John Welch/The Many Press
John Wilkinson
Tim Woods
The Word Hoard
Anonymous x 9